Linda O'Grady
Kristina Riess

FROM THE BÜRGERAMT TO THE BEDROOM

Your essential guide to moving to Germany

We love hearing from our readers! Please send your thoughts or feedback to the following email address and we'll get back to you as soon as we can.

Email: buergeramttobedroom@gmail.com

A NOTE ON THE AUTHORS

Originally from Ireland, Linda O'Grady moved to Berlin almost five years ago, having previously lived in Poland and Latvia. She works as an English teacher, writer and translator.

Kristina Riess is the owner of a small language school in Berlin and the author of easy-to-read books for German learners. She grew up in a small seaside village, but nevertheless has managed to survive life in the big city. So far.

Content:

Foreword

First of all, a big hearty welcome to Germany! Maybe you already speak a little German, maybe not. Either way, relax - this book will help you through those first few days or weeks, when everything is new, and most things are in a language you don't understand (with words as long as your arm).

As a foreigner here myself, I'd been thinking about what I would have appreciated when I first moved to Berlin and knew exactly two sentences in German – "My name is Linda" and "Do you speak English?" Needless to say, that didn't get me very far.

I was lucky enough to make a couple of German friends who I drove mad with questions, but they obviously couldn't be with me all the time, much to their great relief I'm sure. What I really needed was a sort of "German in my pocket" - someone who could answer my questions, tell me the right way to say something, and basically just guide me through everything from scaling the German wall of bureaucracy to figuring out which pizza toppings I was ordering. Kristina and I were looking for a German-English project we could work on together and that's how we came up with the idea for this book.

Of course, translation tools were a huge help in the beginning and there's a vast amount of online information out there, but this book has been lovingly written with the aim of bringing all of that together in one easy-to-access place.

We've kept the structure simple with FAQs and practical vocabulary you can flick back and forth to depending on the situation you're in. For those who want to push themselves a bit more, there's a short test at the end of each chapter and we've also included a section with useful websites. Anecdotes from other expats here show that everything *is* doable and, even if you do make a few clangers along the way (highly likely), you'll get there in the end.

Linda O'Grady

I would also like to welcome you to Germany! *Willkommen in Deutschland!*

As a German teacher, I've met a lot of foreigners from all over the world. In addition to teaching the language, I also consider it part of my job to help my students adapt to their new home by answering their questions and explaining all the strange little things that are new to them here. Often I realize that something that seems very normal and reasonable to me (of course I have five different trash cans in my kitchen!) might not be that way for everyone – or, as in the case of our wonderful German bureaucracy, might not be reasonable at all.

Linda and I approached this project from two different angles. While she knew the problems a foreigner has to face first-hand, I was able to add the German perspective. By combining the two, we have hopefully put together a helpful guide with the answers to your most pressing questions - at least until you're able to manage everything by yourself.

I hope that, whatever your reasons for coming here, you'll get along well and have a great time! Please don't be discouraged if you experience a bit of friction early on, or if things get more complicated than expected. That's just a normal part of learning to live in a new country. Stick with it, and soon enough you'll be wondering how you ever survived without your daily *Brötchen*, your weekly *Tatort*, or your hourly *Ritter Sport* chocolate.

Kristina Riess

So, if you're ready to begin your new life here in this wonderful country, let's get started!

INTRODUCTION TO PHONETICS

This book will help you out a lot when you first get here but there's only so much it can do - it won't actually "teach" you German. If you want to speak, understand, and have a conversation, it won't replace language classes. Of course, everything will be much easier when you do speak (a bit of) the language. Until then, the useful phrases and vocabulary in this book will guide you through the various adventures you're going to have, many of which will happen quite early on during your time in Germany.

In order to use the vocabulary, to understand it when spoken to, and actively produce the phrases, you'll need a brief explanation on how to pronounce German words.

Fortunately, for the most part, German pronunciation is pretty straightforward; if the letter is there, you say it. There's a consistency to German that doesn't exist in English - just think of the words "thought," "though," "bough" and "enough," for example. The German language, a bit like the people, is more direct. You'll find a detailed phonetics chart at the back of the book.

CHAPTER 1
The basics
Die Grundlagen

The Germans may not be the smiliest people on the planet, but once you get to know them a bit, you'll find they're a friendly, helpful bunch. Anything from locating the nearest post office to searching for an apartment, the locals will be your best bet. And speaking a few words *auf Deutsch* never hurts.

Sure, it can be hard going from "hero" in your native language - smart, charming, funny - to "zero" in German, but watching a table full of Germans keel over laughing as you earnestly translate directly from your mother tongue is a win in its own way. As a lot of people move to Germany expecting everyone to speak perfect English, the Germans are generally delighted when you make any sort of effort - even if you do make a bit of an *Arsch* of yourself in the beginning.

And of course, it works both ways - keeping a straight face while your new German buddy tells you that you should probably put your *hand shoes* on as it's a bit chilly outside will be your reward.

So, keep trying, keep laughing, don't get too bogged down with "*der, die, das*" - a mumbled "d" sound might save your sanity - and it'll get a little easier every day. For now, here are a few handy phrases and explanations to get you started.

FAQ:

How do I say "Hello" and "Goodbye"?
There are many regional variations to greet someone or say goodbye, but the ones that will be understood throughout the country are "*Hallo*" as a slightly casual greeting, the more official "*guten Tag*" (good day) and "*guten Abend*" (good evening). "*Guten Morgen*" (good morning) or just "*Morgen*" is also used in informal situations.
"Bye" is "*Tschüss*" - normally said in an extremely high-pitched voice - or more formally, "*Auf Wiedersehen*" (Goodbye, until we see each other again).

When and how do I use "How are you?"
The German equivalent to "How are you?" is "*Wie geht's?*" (literally: "How's it going?") which is the shortened form of "*Wie geht es dir?*" for a friend and "*Wie geht es Ihnen?*," which is more formal. But "How are you?" isn't just an empty question to be thrown around. No, in Germany, small talk is taken seriously - if a German asks you this, they're genuinely interested so feel free to be as long-winded as possible when you answer - tell them about your problems with your neighbors, Grandma's latest illness or how the awful weather is getting you down.

Of course, it's also fine to just give a short answer; "*gut, danke*" (good, thanks) would be the safe option but why not amaze and impress your new pals by using more colorful expressions like "*großartig*" (great), "*super*" or "*hervorragend*" (exceptional). It's also perfectly acceptable to answer honestly "*nicht so gut*" (not very well) or even "*schlecht*" (bad) but be prepared to elaborate if you do.

If you're answering in a full sentence, you say "*Mir geht es gut*" or "*Es geht mir gut*" (It's going well for me) and NOT "*Ich bin gut*" (I am good). This means you're good at something or just a great person in general (which might also be true but is probably not what you meant). If you want to return the question, the right way is "*Und dir?*" (And you?) for a friend, and "*Und Ihnen?*" in more formal situations.

What does "*na?*" mean?
For a nation that adores ridiculously long words, the Germans can also be surprisingly brief. Often you will just hear the word "*na?*". If you're looking for something quick to say to a person without having to listen to their life story, this is the best option. Germans use it all the time and it just means "I notice you're here" or "We know each other and are friendly." It can be used in passing or as a starter to a conversation. It's common to call a friend, say your name and then "na?" (with a rising intonation). The other person then answers the same way, "*na?*" (again with a rising intonation). Never forget to respond - an unanswered "*na?*" is a sad and lonely thing and the other person will forever wonder what they did to upset you...

What's the difference between "*du*" and "*Sie*"?
"*Sie*" is the formal, respectful "you" to address an adult that you don't know or are not friends with (it shows respect, not necessarily distance)."*Du*" is the informal word for "you" and is used for friends, children or people in certain social groups (like students at university, even if they don't know each other).

For example:

What's your name?	*Wie heißen Sie?* (formal)
	Wie heißt du? (informal)

It's not unusual for older people to still *siezen* (this is the verb meaning "to say Sie to someone" which would probably be something like "you-ing" in English...) their co-workers of 30 years although in modern companies this has become less common.

Basically, if in doubt, choose "*Sie*". That way you won't offend anyone and the other person can always tell you that it's okay to *duzen* (say "*du*" to me).

Do Germans say "Nice to meet you"?
Not really, it sounds very official. The correct greeting would be "*Schön, Sie kennenzulernen*" or more familiarly "*Schön, dich kennenzulernen*" but unless you're meeting the Chancellor, you probably won't need either version. Instead just smile and nod.

Why do Germans stare?
They just do. Stare back - you'll feel more like a local.

Expat story:
"One day, I decided I was finally going to ignore the rude (in Germany: normal) stares of passersby. I was feeling pretty good about myself only to realize a short while later that my fly was down. Of course, it wasn't just a little zipper hidden under a shirt. No, I was wearing high-waisted shorts with my shirt tucked in and a full 6 inches of wide-open fabric and my belly sticking out for the whole world to see!"
Sarah, Canada

Useful vocabulary:

Hello	Hallo
Good morning	(Guten) Morgen
Good day	Guten Tag
Good evening	Guten Abend
Good night	Gute Nacht
Bye	Tschüss
Goodbye	Auf Wiedersehen
How are you / How's it going?	Wie geht es Ihnen? (formal)
	Wie geht's? (abbreviation, informal)
Is everything okay?	Alles gut / klar / okay?
Yes / No	ja / nein (informal: nee)
Have a nice day	Schönen Tag
Have a nice evening	Schönen Abend
Have a nice weekend	Schönes Wochenende
You too / same to you	gleichfalls, ebenfalls, ebenso, auch so (both formal and informal)
	Ihnen auch! (formal)
	Dir auch! (informal)
See you tomorrow / soon	Bis morgen / bald
Sorry / Excuse me	Entschuldigung
I'm sorry	Es tut mir Leid
Please / You're welcome / There you go	bitte
Thank you	danke
My pleasure / with pleasure	gern(e)
Thank you very much	vielen Dank
I don't speak German.	Ich spreche kein Deutsch.
I don't understand	Ich verstehe nicht.
Could you repeat that, please?	Wiederholen, bitte.
Say it again, please.	Noch einmal, bitte.
Excuse me / say it again	Wie bitte?
Do you speak English?	Sprechen Sie Englisch?
What's your name?	Wie heißen Sie? (formal)
	Wie heißt du? (informal)
My name is…	Ich heiße… / Mein Name ist….
Where are you from?	Woher kommen Sie? (formal)
	Woher kommst du? (informal)
I'm from… .	Ich komme aus…

Test yourself
The basics

Die Grundlagen

1. Hallo, wie geht's dir?

a. Wie geht's?
b. Danke.
c. Es geht mir gut und dir?
d. Nicht so gut und Ihnen?

2. Guten Tag, wie geht es Ihnen?

a. Danke gut und Ihnen?
b. Ich bin gut.
c. Gut und Sie?
d. Na?

3. Schönen Abend!

a. Wie geht's?
b. Gleichfalls
c. Schönen Abend!
d. Auf Wiedersehen

4. Woher kommst du?

a. Danke gut und Ihnen?
b. Ich komme aus Spanien.
c. Ebenso
d. Woher kommen Sie?

5. Vielen Dank

a. Ihnen auch
b. Ich spreche kein Deutsch.
c. Entschuldigung
d. Gern

6. Sprechen Sie Deutsch?

a. Entschuldigung
b. Gern
c. Nein, ich spreche kein Deutsch.
d. Ich komme aus Indien.

Answers: 1c, 2a, 3b, 4b, 5d, 6c

CHAPTER 2
Numbers, times and dates
Zahlen, Uhrzeiten und Datum

Expat story:
"My daughters and I are trying to learn German. We've just completed our A1.1 course and next week we move on to A1.2. This essentially means that we are now able to tell people our names, where we are from, and that we speak English 'und ein bisschen Deutsch'. We can also count... sort of. I feel fairly confident saying my numbers up to nineteen, and then I have to stop. The German number for 20 is zwanzig. This seems simple enough, however, for some reason I tend to say another word - schwanzig. It sounds similar to my ear. The meaning is NOT similar. 'Schwanz' in German means tail but it's also a slang word for penis and while the word schwanzig doesn't exist, if it did, it would mean something like 'penis-like'. Not the best word to say when at the grocery store and trying to communicate with the clerk. Hi, my name is Cherie and I would like penis-like tomatoes, please, or I would like penis-like Brötchen, bitte. So many new ways for me to embarrass myself..."
Cherie, USA

As you can see, it's probably a good idea to be able to say and understand numbers early on; they'll likely be one of the first things you encounter here in Germany.

Whether it's being told how much you have to pay at the supermarket, hearing an announcement for a last-minute change of train platform, or arranging a time to meet your new German best friend, you'll need to figure out those figures. You'll also have to say your building number, post code and date of birth **a lot** during your various dances with German bureaucracy.

In the beginning, this will require your brain to make some Yoda-style manoeuvres - training yourself to say "seven and thirty" instead of "thirty-seven" won't happen overnight but it will happen sooner rather than later with a bit of practice. Yes, train and practice you must... In the meantime, here are some handy hints to get you started. You'll also find useful vocabulary for making appointments in this chapter.

Numbers

0 - null			
1 - eins	11 - elf	10 - zehn	100 - (ein)hundert
2 - zwei / (zwo*)	12 - zwölf	20 - zwanzig	1000 - (ein)tausend
3 - drei	13 - dreizehn	30 - dreißig	
4 - vier	14 - vierzehn	40 - vierzig	
5 - fünf	15 - fünfzehn	50 - fünfzig	
6 - sech**s**	16 - **sech**zehn	60 - **sech**zig	
7 - sieb**en**	17 - **sieb**zehn	70 - **sieb**zig	
8 - acht	18 - achtzehn	80 - achtzig	
9 - neun	19 - neunzehn	90 - neunzig	

(*_zwo_: sometimes used to avoid confusion with "_drei_," for example when giving phone numbers)

So far, so normal. But now on to the weird part - in German, you say two-digit numbers back to front.

21	einundzwanzig (one and twenty)
48	achtundvierzig (eight and forty)

For three- or more-digit numbers, you only read the last two digits this way.

286	zweihundertsechsundachtzig (two hundred, six and eighty)
5497	fünftausendvierhundertsiebenundneunzig (five thousand, four hundred, seven and ninety - and yes, it's really all one word)

It might look intimidating but just remember to break down the massive words into manageable chunks.
fünf-tausend-vier-hundert-sieben-und-neunzig

Time of the day

There's an official and a more casual way to express the time. The official one is easier because it's mostly just numbers. It uses the 24-hour clock and will always be accompanied by the word "_Uhr_" (o'clock). It's common to use it when talking to friends so you can just stick with that. But you'll also hear the casual form quite a bit so it's useful to at least be able to understand it. The casual method only uses the 12-hour clock.

Official:

8.00	acht Uhr	19.25	neunzehn Uhr fünfundzwanzig
10.05	zehn Uhr fünf	21.58	einundzwanzig Uhr achtundfünfzig

Casual:

8.00	acht	8.40	zwanzig vor neun
8.05	fünf nach acht	8.45	Viertel vor neun
8.10	zehn nach acht	8.50	zehn vor neun
8.15	Viertel nach acht	8.55	fünf vor neun
8.20	zwanzig nach acht	8.58	kurz vor neun / fast neun / or simply: neun
8.25	fünf vor halb neun	9.02	kurz nach neun
8.30	halb neun	13.00	eins
8.35	fünf nach halb neun	21.00	neun

Useful vocabulary:

after / past	nach
before / to	vor
quarter	Viertel
half	halb
short(ly)	kurz
almost	fast
a.m. (about 5 - 9 a.m.)	morgens
a.m. (about 9 - 12 p.m.)	vormittags
p.m. (about 12 - 2 p.m.)	mittags
p.m. (about 2 - 6 p.m.)	nachmittags
p.m. (about 6 - 11 p.m.)	abends
p.m. (after 11 p.m.)	nachts

Note: be careful with half hours - in English, half nine is half past nine (9.30). In German, half nine (*halb neun*) is half past eight (8.30). You don't want to be showing up everywhere an hour late - punctuality is valued pretty highly here…

Dates

In German, ordinal numbers are used for the date. Note that they can also be used to replace the name of the month (January = first (month), February = second (month) and so on).

on January first

am ersten Januar
am ersten ersten

on July 24th

am vierundzwanzigsten Juli
am vierundzwanzigsten siebten

Dates are written like this: 01.01.2020

2nd	zweiten
3rd	**drit**ten
4th	vierten
5th	fünften
6th	sechsten
7th	**sieb**ten
8th	achten
9th	neunten
10th	zehnten
11th	elften
12th	zwölften
13th	dreizehnten
14th	vierzehnten
15th	fünfzehnten
16th	**sech**zehnten
17th	**sieb**zehnten
18th	achtzehnten
19th	neunzehnten
20th, 21st...	zwanzigsten, einundzwanzigsten…
30th, 31st	dreißigsten, einunddreißigsten
January	Januar
February	Februar
March	März
April	April
May	Mai
June	Juni
July	Juli
August	August
September	September

October	Oktober
November	November
December	Dezember
1995	neunzehnhundertfünfundneunzig
2019	zweitausendneunzehn

Useful vocabulary:

Appointment	Termin
Day	Tag
Time of the day	Uhrzeit
Date	Datum
Place	Ort
Address	Adresse
When	wann
Yesterday	gestern
Today	heute
Tomorrow	morgen
at (8 o'clock)	um (8 Uhr)
(on) Monday	(am) Montag
(on) Tuesday	(am) Dienstag
(on) Wednesday	(am) Mittwoch
(on) Thursday	(am) Donnerstag
(on) Friday	(am) Freitag
(on) Saturday	(am) Samstag / (am) Sonnabend
(on) Sunday	(am) Sonntag
(at the) weekend	(am) Wochenende
Last / this / next week	letzte / diese / nächste Woche
Last / this / next month	letzten / diesen / nächsten Monat
Last / this / next year	letztes / dieses / nächstes Jahr
In the morning (about 5 - 9 a.m.)	am Morgen
In the morning (about 9 - 12 p.m.)	am Vormittag
In the middle of the day (about 12 - 2 p.m.)	am Mittag
In the afternoon (about 2 - 6 p.m.)	am Nachmittag
In the evening (about 6 - 11 p.m.)	am Abend
At night (about 11 p.m. - 5 a.m.)	in der Nacht
Urgent	dringend
Emergency	Notfall
I'd like to make an appointment.	Ich möchte einen Termin machen.
Unfortunately I'll have to cancel / postpone the appointment.	Leider muss ich den Termin absagen / verschieben.
I have an / no appointment.	Ich habe einen / keinen Termin.
When can I come?	Wann kann ich kommen?
At what time?	Um wie viel Uhr?
I don't have time then.	Da habe ich keine Zeit.
I can't.	Ich kann nicht.
Are you available on Monday?	Können Sie am Montag?

Is it possible?	Ist es möglich?
I'm available on Monday / at 8 o'clock.	Ich kann am Montag / um 8 Uhr.
Is earlier possible?	Geht es früher?
That works.	Das passt.
It's very urgent / not so urgent.	Es ist sehr dringend / nicht so dringend.
It can wait.	Es hat Zeit. / Es kann warten.
What's your address?	Wie ist Ihre Adresse?
Can I bring my children?	Kann ich meine Kinder mitbringen?
Do I have to bring anything else?	Muss ich sonst noch etwas mitbringen?
When's your birthday?	Wann haben Sie Geburtstag?
My birthday is on March 5th.	Mein Geburtstag ist am 5. (fünften) März.

Test yourself
Numbers, times and dates
Zahlen, Uhrzeiten und Datum

1. Ich möchte einen Termin machen.

a. Ist das Restmüll?
b. Wie viele?
c. Ist die Küche groß?
d. Können Sie am Montag?

2. Leider muss ich den Termin absagen.

a. Am Montag?
b. Das kostet 100 Euro.
c. Möchten Sie einen neuen Termin?
d. Der Termin ist heute.

3. Möchten Sie den Termin diese Woche?

a. In der Nacht.
b. Ich habe ein Ticket.
c. Ja, es ist dringend.
d. Nein, der Termin ist um 8.

4. Um 14 Uhr?

a. Ja, das passt.
b. Um 14 Uhr kommt die Müllabfuhr.
c. Nein, ich bin nicht katholisch.
d. Ich habe keinen Termin.

5. Um wie viel Uhr?

a. Am Montag.
b. Am Wochenende.
c. Um 13 Uhr.
d. Heute.

6. Ist Montag okay für Sie?

a. Nein, da habe ich keine Zeit.
b. Gibt es eine Einbauküche?
c. Es ist besser am Vormittag.
d. Nein, ich habe keine Haustiere.

Answers: 1d, 2c, 3c, 4a, 5c, 6a

CHAPTER 3
<u>Finding an apartment</u>
Eine Wohnung finden

An interesting quirk of the Germans is that when they move apartment, they take everything with them - sometimes right down to the lighting fixtures and sockets. The expression "everything but the kitchen sink" could have originated in Germany as that's one of the few things they leave behind - in Berlin, at any rate.

In the capital, by law, every kitchen has to have a cooker and a sink; in other states, only the water, gas and electricity outlets are provided. So, a word to the wise: if you're looking for a place with a fitted kitchen, make sure that it specifically says "*EBK*" (*Einbauküche*) in the listing. "But wouldn't it be easier if everyone just left the fittings behind so the next tenant didn't have to bring all of their fittings with them - and the next, and the next...?" you ask. You'd think so but, for a lovably logical people, this one seems to have passed the Germans by.

If the thought of trying to find and furnish an entire apartment seems a little daunting at this stage, one way to ease yourself into German living is to get a room in a shared apartment for a few months. This is known as a "*WG*" (pronounced "veh geh"), probably because "*Wohngemeinschaft*" is too long to say. All the better if you can find a place with German housemates so you can wow them with your newfound German language skills.

You'll also learn useful life skills like folding a pizza box to around the size of a matchbox before putting it in the trash, how to clean things that are already clean, and the correct way to boil an egg. Yup, chances are you've been doing it wrong your whole life. Don't worry, the Germans are here to help with their (usually quite dizzying) array of German household gadgets.

<u>FAQ:</u>

What's the best way to find an apartment in Germany?
You'll find a list of the most popular rental websites at the back of the book. Bear in mind that it can take anywhere from a few weeks to several months to find a place, especially in the big cities, so just keep at it. The *WG*-option can be a good place to start, just to buy yourself some

time while you get organized. Other short-term options are Airbnb and serviced apartments, though these are obviously more expensive. Talk to people, keep an ear to the ground and an eye on social media sites - you'll find somewhere eventually.

How many rooms does a 1-room apartment really have?
In Germany, one room actually means one room - unlike in many countries it's not just the bedrooms that are counted and the living room is always extra. The bathroom and the kitchen (which may or may not be separate) are not included in the room count. The entire livable area is measured in square meters.

How much should I earn to rent an apartment?
The rule of thumb is three times the "cold" rent (*Kaltmiete*).

What's the standard deposit?
Legally not more than three times the *Kaltmiete* (and usually exactly that).

What documents will I need to show?
This might vary slightly from landlord to landlord but it's a good idea to have the following documents to hand:
- Passport / ID
- Your last three payslips (freelancers might have to get a statement of income from a tax advisor)
- Previous address registration document (if you have one)
- *Schufa-Auskunft* - credit rating report (you can order this online so please see the list of websites at the back of the book). A credit rating report from your home country might also be accepted.
- *Mietschuldenfreiheitsbescheinigung* - a statement from your previous landlord that you paid your rent in full and on time
- (less likely) *Haftpflichtversicherungsnachweis* - proof of personal liability insurance
  (Have fun saying those last two…)

Should I transfer any money without seeing the apartment first?
Absolutely not. There are a lot of scammers out there so if it looks too good to be true, then it probably is. If you get a reply along these lines, run like the wind:

> *Hello,*
> *It's great that you're interested in my apartment! My name is blah blah and I currently live in (insert random country here). As it would cost quite a lot for me to come back to (insert German city here) to show the apartment, I need to know that you are a serious tenant. Therefore, I ask you to transfer €... and I will post you the keys so you can view the property. This will all be done through Airbnb so we know we can trust each other...*

Airbnb do not offer a service like this and you will never see your money again. You have been warned.

Who will help me if I have problems with my landlord?
Unfortunately, landlords are not always the most honest people and are often known for trying to cheat their tenants to make some extra cash - foreigners who don't know the local customs can be easy victims. So, if you're surprised to receive a €1,000 heating bill and the landlord tells you that's it's perfectly normal and you have to pay it, you might want to have this checked by a third party. *Miet(er)vereine* (tenant associations) are your best option. These associations help tenants in many ways - they explain laws, give legal counseling, help to write letters and so on. You have to become a member (membership fees are around €80 per year) but then you can contact them for free advice whenever needed. Membership is recommended especially if you don't speak the language (well), but you don't need to get it right away - it's enough to reach out to them and become a member when you actually have a problem. You'll find the link to their website at the back of the book.

Useful vocabulary:

Apartment	Wohnung
House	Haus
Building	Gebäude
To rent	mieten
Rent for a house or apartment exclusive of heating and other costs	Kaltmiete
Rent for a house or apartment including additional costs	Warmmiete
Additional costs	Nebenkosten
Heating costs	Heizkosten
Electricity	Strom
Water	Wasser
Total rent	Gesamtmiete
Habitable space	Wohnfläche
1-room, 2-room apartment	1-Zimmer-Wohnung, 2-Zimmer-Wohnung
1st, 2nd, 2rd, 4th, 5th floor	1. (erste), 2. (zweite), 3. (dritte), 4. (vierte), 5. (fünfte) Etage
	1. (erster), 2. (zweiter), 3. (dritter), 4. (vierter), 5. (fünfter) Stock
Building built before 1949	Altbau
Building built after 1949	Neubau
(Partly) furnished	(teilweise) möbliert
Elevator	Aufzug / Fahrstuhl
Balcony	Balkon
Terrace	Terrasse
Basement	Keller
Garage / parking space	Garage / Stellplatz
Bedroom	Schlafzimmer
Bathroom (with a window)	Badezimmer (mit Fenster)
Hall	Flur
Stairs	Treppe
Shower	Dusche
Bathtub	Badewanne
Kitchen	Küche
Fitted kitchen	Einbauküche
Sink	Spüle
Floor	(Fuß)Boden
Wood	Holz

Heating	Heizung
Stove	Herd
Oven	Ofen
Beautiful	schön
Bright	hell
Spacious	geräumig
Courtyard facing	zum Hof
Street facing	zur Straße
Modernized / renovated	modernisiert / renoviert / saniert
Viewing appointment	Besichtigungstermin
Move (noun)	Umzug
Move (verb)	umziehen
Moving company	Umzugsfirma
Moving boxes	Umzugskartons
Dear...	Sehr geehrte Damen und Herren (neutral) / Sehr geehrte Frau... (for a woman) / Sehr geehrter Herr... (for a man)
I've seen this apartment on ...	Ich habe die Wohnung am... besichtigt.
I like the apartment very much.	Die Wohnung gefällt mir sehr.
I'm very interested.	Ich bin sehr interessiert.
I'd like to see the apartment.	Ich möchte die Wohnung besichtigen.
I'm free on the ...	Ich habe Zeit am...
Can you let me know if this suits you?	Bitte teilen Sie mir mit, ob Ihnen das passt.
Thank you for getting back to me.	Vielen Dank für Ihre Rückmeldung.
Thank you for your quick reply.	Vielen Dank für Ihre schnelle Antwort.
Please find my documents attached.	Sie finden meine Unterlagen im Anhang.
What's the rent?	Wie hoch ist die Miete?
Does this include all additional costs?	Sind alle Nebenkosten inklusive?
How much are the additional costs?	Wie hoch sind die Nebenkosten?
Is there a deposit?	Gibt es eine Kaution?
How much is the deposit?	Wie hoch ist die Kaution?
When can I sign the contract?	Wann kann ich den Vertrag unterschreiben?
Can you send me the contract?	Können Sie mir den Vertrag schicken?

Sample email of interest:

Sehr geehrte Damen und Herren,

mit großem Interesse habe ich Ihre Wohnungsanzeige gelesen. Ich, Peter Smith (29 Jahre, Informatiker, verheiratet, zwei Kinder), würde mich sehr über eine Einladung zu einem Besichtigungstermin freuen. Sie erreichen mich unter der Telefonnummer 0170 - 123 456 78 oder unter peter.smith@internet.com.

Mit freundlichen Grüßen
Peter Smith

Dear Sir / Madam,

I read the advertisement for your apartment with great interest. I'm Peter Smith (29 years old, a computer scientist, married with two children) and I would be very pleased to receive an invitation to view the apartment. You can reach me by telephone at 0170 - 123 456 78 or at peter.smith@internet.com.

Best regards,
Peter Smith.

Test yourself
Finding an apartment
Eine Wohnung finden

1. Wie hoch ist die Miete?

a. Holzfußboden
b. Können Sie mir sagen, ob Ihnen das passt?
c. 700 Euro plus Nebenkosten
d. Teilweise möbliert

2. Sind die Nebenkosten inklusive?

a. Nur die Heizkosten
b. Die Wohnung ist möbliert.
c. Es ist Altbau.
d. Die Wohnung hat einen Balkon.

3. Ist die Wohnung möbliert?

a. Die Wohnung hat ein Badezimmer mit Fenster.
b. Teilweise
c. Die Miete ist 500 Euro.
d. Die Heizkosten sind extra.

4. Hat die Wohnung eine Einbauküche?

a. Ja, sie ist zum Hof gelegen.
b. Die Heizkosten sind inklusive.
c. Nein, leider nicht.
d. Nein, es ist kein Altbau.

5. Wie hoch ist die Kaution?

a. Die Terrasse
b. Neubau von 1975
c. Hell und schön
d. Zwei Monatsmieten

6. Sind Sie interessiert?

a. Nein, gerne
b. Vielen Dank für Ihre Rückmeldung.
c. Ja, sehr
d. Die Wohnung hat eine Garage.

Answers: 1c, 2a, 3b, 4c, 5d, 6c

CHAPTER 4
At the Bürgeramt
Im Bürgeramt

Now that you've got a roof over your head, if you want to live like a real person and do important stuff such as get WiFi and a smartphone (and trivialities like a bank account and tax number), you need to register your address. This all-important piece of paper is called a "*Meldebescheinigung*" – try saying that drunk. In order to get this, you have to go to a *Bürgeramt*, or in some regions an *Einwohnermeldeamt* (citizens' center), to register.

Up until this point, you may have thought of Germany as the land of shiny efficiency; the *Bürgeramt* experience will cure you of this notion pretty quickly.

One way to get your *Meldebescheinigung* is to get up at around 4 a.m. and go to the center a couple of hours before it opens. There will probably already be a line of roughly fifty sleepy people ahead of you and, after around half an hour, another hundred and fifty behind you. The latter will be sleepy and angry because they didn't get up half an hour earlier.

When the doors open, run to the reception desk and take a number. Try to keep yourself entertained in the waiting room by watching all of the hopeful heads bobbing up and down like meerkats every time a new number pops up on the screen - "ping!" You might not even realize that you're one of the meerkats and someone else is watching you - classic *Bürgeramt* fun.

However, if you value sleep and not spending the best part of your day in a sad waiting room, the smarter way is to make an appointment. You can do this online so you don't have to speak to a scary German paper-pusher on the phone.

The charming individuals who work at the *Bürgerämter* have been known to reduce even the most hardened expats to blubbering wrecks in the space of around two minutes but, oh, the joy, the sheer joy of it when you get a person who actually likes their job - and other human beings. It has been known to happen and you could be the lucky one. Walking out of the *Bürgeramt* with a smile on your face might seem like a small victory but it's one that you'll probably be telling your grandkids about in years to come.

But why, you ask, can't I do all of this online? Because, well, no. Welcome to Germany.

FAQ:

How do I make an appointment?
To make an appointment online, please see the list of websites at the back of the book. If you're feeling brave, dial 115 (nationwide).

Do I have to register at the nearest *Bürgeramt*?
No, if you live in one of the bigger cities, you can register in any district. Just do a city-wide search for available appointments. Usually it's easier to get one at a Bürgeramt a bit further out from the center.

Do I need to pay to register?
Nope, registration is free just like all of the best things in life…

If I move, can I re-register online?
Ha ha. No.

What documents do I need to bring with me?
Your passport / ID, a completed *Anmeldung* (registration) form and a *Wohnungsgeberbestätigung*, which is a signed confirmation from your landlord that you live at the address. You can download these forms online.

(Note: required documents may vary from state to state. Be sure to check before you go as this is not a process you want to have to repeat.)

Will they speak English at the *Bürgeramt*?
Highly unlikely and there's a good chance they'll yell at you for even asking. If you're lucky, you won't have to say much as all of the information should be on the form or your ID. If you're unlucky, they might just point at random words and shout them at you - repeatedly. "*Es steht da, oder…?*" (It's written there, right?) and a vague gesture at your paperwork is your friend in this case. Alternatively, bring along a real live German - some even offer this service professionally.

Why does it matter what religion I am?
In Germany, there's a church tax if you're a member of certain religions - it amounts to 8% to 9% of your annual income tax. Leaving the religion box on the form blank is an option, but there's a good chance that

German bureaucracy will come after you anyway and charge you back taxes - they assume that if you're from a certain country, you're a certain religion. For example, Irish = Roman Catholic. If you receive a *"Feststellung der Zugehörigkeit zu einer öffentlich-rechtlichen Religionsgemeinschaft"* - catchy - in the mail after registration, you will have to officially leave the church to avoid paying this tax.

Depending on the state, you can do this at the *Amtsgericht* (district court) or the *Standesamt* (registration office) - and you will have to pay for the pleasure. Fees vary from state to state. You'll also need to keep the confirmation document forever as the *Amtsgericht* only keeps a copy for 10 years, so if they decide to check 20 years from now and you can't produce the document, you'll be charged back taxes. (As a general rule, keep every piece of paper forever - you never know when German bureaucracy will come back and bite you in the you know what.)

What if I decide to leave Germany?
Well, hopefully you won't decide to leave just yet, but if you do plan on leaving the country (for an extended period or permanently), then you will need to "de-register" by getting an *Abmeldebescheinigung*. Just go back to the *Bürgeramt* to get it. It will be useful and sometimes even necessary for canceling contracts (gym, phone, etc.) early. If you're moving within the country, you don't need to de-register; just register again at your new address

.

Useful vocabulary:

Citizens' center	Bürgeramt / Einwohnermeldeamt
New apartment	Neue Wohnung
New residence	Neue Wohnsitz
Previous residence	Bisheriger Wohnsitz
Sole residence	Alleiniger Wohnsitz
Main residence	Hauptwohnsitz
Secondary residence	Nebenwohnsitz
Move-in date	Tag des Einzugs
Postal code	Postleitzahl (PLZ)
Street, house number	Straße, Hausnummer (Haus-Nr.)
Surname / Family name	Familienname / Nachname
First name(s)	Vorname(n)
Maiden name	Geburtsname / Mädchenname
Gender	Geschlecht
Male	männlich
Female	weiblich
Date, location, country of birth	Tag, Ort, Land der Geburt / Geburtstag, Geburtsort
Religion	Religion
Citizenship	Staatsangehörigkeit
Religious order or artist's name	Ordens- oder Künstlername
Marital status	Familienstand
Married	verheiratet
Divorced	geschieden
Not married	ledig
Widowed	verwitwet
Date, signature	Datum, Unterschrift

I'd like to register my new apartment.	Ich möchte meine neue Wohnung anmelden.
I moved in on the …	Ich bin am … eingezogen.
Here is my passport and documents	Hier sind mein Pass und meine Unterlagen.
Do I need to sign anything?	Muss ich etwas unterschreiben?
Do you need a signature?	Brauchen Sie eine Unterschrift?
I'm sorry, I don't understand	Es tut mir leid, ich verstehe nicht.
Can I google that?	Darf ich das googeln?
I'd like to de-register.	Ich möchte mich abmelden.
Will I get a confirmation?	Bekomme ich eine Bescheinigung?
Have a nice (rest of your) day.	Schönen Tag (noch).
Thank you very much for your help.	Vielen Dank für Ihre Hilfe.

Test yourself
At the Bürgeramt
Im Bürgeramt

1. Ich möchte meine neue Wohnung anmelden.

a. Nein, ich spreche kein Englisch.
b. Sind Sie Peter Smith?
c. Wann sind Sie eingezogen?
d. Mit Nebenkosten?

2. Wann Sind Sie eingezogen?

a. In der Müllerstraße
b. Am 5. Oktober
c. Aus Schweden
d. Nein, danke

3. Was ist Ihr Familienstand?

a. Ich bin Ingenieur.
b. Ich bin verheiratet.
c. Ich bin sehr groß.
d. Ich bin katholisch.

4. Muss ich etwas unterschreiben?

a. Nein, am Mittwoch
b. Ja, 20 Euro
c. Ja, hier
d. Nein, sie haben kein Ticket.

5. Was ist Ihre Staatsangehörigkeit?

a. Japanisch
b. Geschieden
c. Weiblich
d. Postleitzahl

6. Was ist Ihre Religion?

a. Vegetarisch
b. Danke, gerne
c. Jüdisch
d. Am Nachmittag

Answers: 1c, 2b, 3b, 4c, 5a, 6c

CHAPTER 5
Opening a bank account
Ein Bankkonto eröffnen

Expat story:

"I'd been in Munich a couple of weeks and was trying to open a bank account. I'd filled in all the papers so was pretty confident when I marched in there. The man asked me for my documents so he could make a copy and when he came back, he said: "Are you related to Fidel Castro?" Erm, what?? "Of course I'm not!" "No, sorry, you can't open a bank account here because of your surname." You can't even imagine my face at that moment - and for several days afterwards!"

Ana Castro Silva, Portugal (where having Castro as a surname is like being a Müller in Germany)

For some, it seems, opening a German bank account is about as much fun as being slapped in the face with a wet fish. Then again, who ever said banking was fun? The good news is that the German banking system is one of the most stable in the world. EU nationals will (usually) have no problems opening a simple German bank account; non-EU nationals will have to prove their registration and provide a valid work permit. They may also be required to keep a certain amount of money in their account as collateral.

There are many German banks to choose from, Deutsche Bank, Commerzbank and Sparkasse being among the biggest. In recent years, purely online banks, such as N26, have also become more popular. However, they are not obliged to open a bank account for you and your application can be rejected without any reason being given.

With most German banks, you still have to go to the bank in person to open an account. There is a chance that you'll be able to deal with someone who speaks English, especially in the bigger cities, although you may need to make an appointment in advance. For all of its progressive ways, Germany is still in many respects a cash culture so make sure that whatever bank you choose has ATMs in your vicinity. If you have a Sparkasse account and withdraw money from a Deutsche Bank machine (or vice versa), you'll be charged a fee that might bring a small tear to your eye. Luckily, most bank machines have the option to switch language so at least you'll see it coming. If you're going to be transferring money to your home country regularly, transfer fees should also be an important deciding factor.

FAQ:

What documents do I need to open an account?
As you've probably started to realize, Germany is a big fan of paperwork and German banks are no exception. In order to open a bank account, you'll need:
- A valid passport / ID
- Your *Meldebescheinigung* (registration document)
- Completed application form
- Initial deposit (the minimum amount depends on the bank)
- Employment contract, payslips (proof of income for freelancers)
- Some banks may also ask for a *Schufa* (credit-rating report)

Will there be fees?
Some accounts are completely free, others demand that you keep a certain minimum amount in your account each month otherwise you'll be charged for services. Sometimes even a transfer may not be free. Make sure to read the terms and conditions carefully - you may need to get a patient German friend to help you with this. Online banks usually don't charge fees.

Can I only use my bank's ATMs?
No, you can use any ATM but if it's not your own bank, there might be charges of between €2 and €6 per withdrawal. If you'd been wondering why your German friend dragged you 5 km out of your way to find a bank machine on a night out, this is why. Some banks do, however, have partner banks so make sure to find out which ATMs are free for you.

How do I get cheques?
You don't - nobody uses cheques anymore. You cannot pay your rent, bills, etc. by cheque; bank transfer is the common method.

Useful vocabulary:

Cash	Bargeld
Account holder	Kontoinhaber
Checking / debit account	Girokonto
Savings account	Sparkonto
Transfer (noun)	Überweisung
Transfer (verb)	überweisen
Cheque	Scheck
Required field (on a form)	Pflichtfeld
Account number	Kontonummer, IBAN
Bank routing code	Bankleitzahl (BLZ), BIC
Interest	Zinsen
Fees	Gebühren
Without fees	gebührenfrei
Deposit	Einzahlung
Withdrawal	Auszahlung
To withdraw money	Geld abheben
Income	Einkommen
Net income	Nettoeinkommen
Salary	Gehalt
Self-employed	selbstständig
Full-time employment	Vollzeit-Anstellung / Vollzeit-Arbeit
Part-time employment	Teilzeit-Anstellung / Teilzeit-Arbeit
Student	Student (male), Studentin (female)
I'd like to open a bank account.	Ich möchte ein Konto eröffnen.
Is there someone here who speaks English?	Spricht jemand Englisch?
Please fill out this form.	Bitte füllen Sie dieses Formular aus.
How much are the monthly fees?	Wie hoch sind die monatlichen Gebühren?
Could you write that down for me?	Können Sie das für mich aufschreiben?
Does the account come with a debit / credit card?	Gibt es eine Bankkarte / Kreditkarte mit diesem Konto?
Can I use this card to shop online?	Kann ich diese Karte benutzen, um online einzukaufen?
Can I do my banking online / on the telephone?	Kann ich Online-Banking / Telefon-Banking benutzen?

Can you give me a demonstration?	Können Sie mir das zeigen?
How much does it cost to make a transfer?	Wie teuer ist eine Überweisung?
When will I get my PIN number?	Wann bekomme ich meine PIN-Nummer?
I've lost my bank card and would like to get a new one.	Ich habe meine Bankkarte verloren und möchte eine neue bekommen.
Have a nice (rest of your) day	Schönen Tag (noch).
Thank you very much for your help.	Vielen Dank für Ihre Hilfe.

Test yourself
Opening a bank account
Ein Bankkonto eröffnen

1. Ich möchte ein Konto eröffnen.

a. Ja, gerne
b. Wie geht's?
c. Entschuldigung
d. 400 Euro plus Nebenkosten

2. Wie hoch sind die monatlichen Gebühren?

a. 10 Minuten
b. 5 Euro
c. 30 Meter
d. 2 Tage

3. Wann bekomme ich meine PIN-Nummer?

a. Bitte füllen Sie das Formular aus.
b. Das Konto ist gebührenfrei.
c. Eine Auszahlung kostet 3 Euro.
d. In der nächsten Woche per Post.

4. Haben Sie ein Einkommen?

a. Ja, ich wohne in Deutschland.
b. Nein, ich spreche kein Englisch.
c. Ja, 2400 Euro netto.
d. Nein, ich arbeite Vollzeit.

5. Kann ich Online-Banking benutzen?

a. Natürlich, das ist gebührenfrei.
b. Nicht am Wochenende.
c. Zwei Monatsmieten
d. Bargeld

6. Gibt es eine Kreditkarte mit diesem Konto?

a. Ja, ich habe Interesse.
b. Vielen Dank für Ihre Rückmeldung.
c. Nein, Sie arbeiten Vollzeit.
d. Ja, aber leider nicht gebührenfrei.

Answers: 1a, 2b, 3d, 4c, 5a, 6d

CHAPTER 6
Health insurance
Krankenversicherung

If there's one thing Germans love - possibly even more than *Schlager** and sausage - it's having insurance. Ask a German what they'd save if their apartment was on fire and, chances are, their insurance documents will be quite high on the list. The Germans are a rather risk-averse people and they feel more relaxed knowing that they're insured against pretty much all eventualities.

Most types of insurance in Germany are optional - *Hunde- / Pferdehaftpflichtversicherung* (Horse / Dog Liability Insurance), *Hausratversicherung* (Home Contents Insurance), *Rechtsschutz-versicherung* (Legal Insurance), *Sterbegeldversicherung* (Death Expenses Insurance), *Risikolebensversicherung* (Life Insurance), *Berufsunfähigkeits-versicherung* (Incapacity To Work Insurance) - the list goes on. Lots of fun to say but it's up to you if you want to take out any of these policies. One that is particularly useful is *Haftpflichtversicherung* (Personal Liability Insurance), which covers the cost of any damages caused by your actions, whether deliberate or not. If you want to see a German horrified, tell them that you don't have *Haftpflichtversicherung* - once you've learned how to say it.

However, the one type of insurance that is compulsory for everyone legally resident in Germany is health insurance - and, as usual, it's complicated.

*Schlager: traditional German music - it will grow on you. Maybe.

FAQ:

What's the difference between public and private health insurance?
The German health system is split into two parts. About 90% of the population have public insurance. Employees are obliged to have it (they get it automatically through their work) and the monthly fees are income-based. The employer pays 50%.
People on a high income (roughly more than €4,500 gross per month) can choose between public and private insurance. The fees for private insurance do not depend on the monthly income but on the age and health status of the individual. It might be a good deal for young and

healthy people whereas switching is not recommended the older one gets (often not recommended after the age of 40), or if there are previous or chronic illnesses. Private insurance companies often have better offers for their clients and cover more treatments. It will also very likely be easier to get appointments with busy specialists. Bear in mind that private insurance companies can reject applications for membership.

How do I get health insurance?

If you are an employee, your company will take care of it for you. If you have a specific insurance that you'd prefer, make sure to talk to HR about it otherwise they will probably just choose the company they normally work with. If you have a high income (over around €5,000 a month) and want to choose private instead of public insurance, talk to HR in advance. They can also register you for public insurance and then your insurance company will inform you that you are entitled to choose.

If you're not in full-time employment, unfortunately it will be difficult for you to get public insurance. Only EU citizens who had public insurance in their home country might qualify. Everyone else (with the exception of artists and freelance publicists, see below) has to get private insurance which can be quite expensive. Make sure to read the contract thoroughly. Many private insurance companies refuse to cover any costs connected to pre-existing conditions or chronic illnesses. You might be able to negotiate a deal that covers everything but this will likely be (much) more expensive.

What does my insurance cover?

Health insurance covers medical costs for doctor's visits, hospitalization, drugs and medical equipment (such as crutches) on prescription. Some insurance might also pay for, or at least subsidize, exercise classes (but only specific certified ones and never gym memberships; check with your insurance company). The cost of new glasses will only be covered if your eyesight is very poor, and professional dental cleaning is also not included. In any case, before getting any treatment, you should check with your doctor if your insurance covers it.

What should I look out for in my contract?

As with all insurance contracts, look at the fees and services, and also the notice period for termination. Pay attention to what the insurance actually covers; your health insurance might not cover every treatment, for example.

Are all public insurance companies the same?
Pretty much. There are slight differences that you might want to check out beforehand (for example, ask which exercise classes they subsidize) but overall they are more or less the same.

Are my children and stay-at-home spouse automatically insured?

Public insurance covers your family (very young children or children in education, and spouses with little or no income) without additional fees (you will have to fill out forms though - of course). This option doesn't exist with private insurance - you'll have to get a separate contract for each family member.

What about special insurance for artists and freelance publicists?
Freelancers and others without employment in Germany have to get private insurance - with one special exemption. The state supports artists and freelance publicists because this occupational group is usually less socially protected than other self-employed people. The "*Künstlersozialkasse*" (artists' social insurance) covers health, pension and care insurance and is very cheap as the state covers 50% of the fees. This insurance only accepts applicants who meet certain criteria. You can check these out on their website (you'll find the link at the back of the book)

Useful vocabulary:

Health insurance	Krankenversicherung / Krankenkasse
Public	gesetzlich
Private	privat
Insurance card	Versichertenkarte
Supplementary insurance	Zusatzversicherung
Take out insurance	eine Versicherung abschließen
Cancel	kündigen
Conditions	Konditionen / Bedingungen
Fees	Gebühren
Contribution	Beitrag
Monthly / yearly	monatlich / jährlich
included	inklusive
What are the fees?	Wie hoch sind die Gebühren?
Will my family be insured automatically?	Ist meine Familie automatisch mitversichert?
How / when will I get my insurance card?	Wie / wann bekomme ich meine Versichertenkarte?
What are the services of this insurance?	Was sind die Leistungen dieser Versicherung?
Will my insurance cover this treatment?	Wird meine Versicherung diese Behandlung übernehmen?
Will this insurance cover treatments abroad?	Wird diese Versicherung auch Behandlungen im Ausland übernehmen?
I've lost my insurance card and would like to get a new one.	Ich habe meine Versichertenkarte verloren und möchte eine neue bekommen.

Test yourself
Health insurance
Krankenversicherung

1. Wie hoch sind die Gebühren?

a. 10 Minuten
b. 90 Euro jährlich
c. 45 Euro in bar
d. Die Gebühren sind nicht hoch.

2. Ist meine Familie automatisch mitversichert?

a. Ja, ihre Frau und ihre Kinder
b. Nein, monatlich sind es 50 Euro
c. Ja, gerne
d. Ja, mit Badewanne

3. Wann bekomme ich meine Versichertenkarte?

a. Nächste Station
b. Nächste Kreuzung links
c. Nächste Woche
d. Der nächste bitte

4. Wird meine Versicherung diese Behandlung übernehmen?

a. Ja, morgen.
b. Nein, das ist leider nicht inklusive.
c. Ja, ihre Kinder sind natürlich mitversichert.
d. Nein, Sie müssen den Beitrag monatlich zahlen.

5. Sind Sie privat versichert?

a. Hier ist meine private Adresse.
b. Ja, ich möchte meine Versicherung kündigen.
c. Ja, ich habe eine Krankenkasse.
d. Nein, gesetzlich.

6. Ich habe meine Versichertenkarte verloren.

a. Kein Problem, möchten Sie eine neue bekommen?
b. Haben Sie eine Zusatzversicherung?
c. Haben Sie ein Einkommen?
d. Danke, gleichfalls.

Answers: 1b, 2a, 3c, 4b, 5d, 6a

CHAPTER 7
Taxes
Steuern

The online tax portal in Germany is called *Elster*. *Elster* means magpie - yep, the bird that has a reputation for stealing your shiny things to line its own nest. And you thought the Germans didn't have a sense of humor...

Apart from that, there's nothing particularly amusing about the German tax system so let's get down to business.

FAQ:

How do I get a tax number?
Foreigners get their tax number (officially called the "*Steueridentifikationsnummer*" or "*Steuer-ID*") after registering at the *Bürgeramt* or *Einwohnermeldeamt* (the name of the *Amt* depends on the state). It should be sent to you by mail shortly after you register. If you don't receive it automatically, you will need to contact your local *Finanzamt* directly. To find your nearest *Finanzamt*, check out the useful links at the back of the book.

Wht are the tax brackets in Germany?
There are six tax brackets (*Steuerklassen*) in Germany, which are based on marital status. The taxes are highest in category 1.
The categories are:

Steuerklasse 1: single, widowed, separated / divorced, married with spouse living abroad
Steuerklasse 2: single parents
Steuerklasse 3: married (spouse with the higher income)
Steuerklasse 4: married (both spouses have the same income)
Steuerklasse 5: married (spouse with the lower income)
Steuerklasse 6: second or part-time job (not related to marital status)

What's the best tax bracket for married people?
If you're married and both working, you will automatically be put in category 4. However, if only one partner works and the other either doesn't work or only has a very small income, you should switch to a

combination of categories 3 and 5 because this will mean lower taxes overall. A change of tax bracket must be requested at the *Finanzamt*.

What are the income tax rates in Germany?

They vary from 14% to 45%; the higher your income, the higher the tax rate. You'll find a link to the various rates at the back of the book.
An example: A gross salary of €3,000 equals €1,960.29 net. The income tax in this case is 34.66% for *Steuerklasse* 1 (2019).

Which charges does the income tax include?
Two types of charges will be deducted from your gross salary.

First, there's the salary tax. Then there's the so-called *Solidaritätsbeitrag* (solidarity surcharge) which is charged to cover the extra costs of German reunification. The *Solidaritätsbeitrag* is 5.5% of your gross salary and it's mandatory. An additional tax is the church tax (*Kirchensteuer*) imposed on members of some religious congregations. It's 8% to 9% of your annual income tax.
The second type of charges are the social security contributions (*Sozialabgaben*). These cover the various insurances: health insurance, pension insurance, care insurance and unemployment insurance.
These charges are mandatory for employees and will be deducted from your gross salary automatically.

What is church tax and do I have to pay it?
The Protestant and Catholic churches, and some Jewish communities can collect church taxes. If you're a member of one of these religious groups, church tax (8 - 9% of your income tax) will be deducted from your gross salary automatically. So how do the German authorities know that you're a member? Well, the official explanation is that churches have baptism registers so, for example, the German Catholic church knows that you were baptised elsewhere therefore making you an official member of the church. This seems to be a very complex method so the more likely explanation is that they often just assume. If you're from Italy, you'll be considered Catholic; if you're from Israel, they'll assume you're Jewish.

The only way to get out of paying this tax is to officially renounce your membership. Depending on the state you live in, you may have to go to the registry office (*Standesamt*) or district court (*Amtsgericht*). It's a quick bureaucratic act that is free in some states but costs up to €100 in others. Even though the office will inform the *Finanzamt* and your employer, make sure you also get a written confirmation. It's not always free but it might be useful in the future because churches can doubt the termination and charge the tax if you don't have proof.

Be careful because renouncing church membership might have consequences for you in your home country.

How does it work for freelancers?
The German tax year is the calendar year. You'll need to file your tax return (*Steuererklärung*) at the *Finanzamt* by May 31st of the following year, or December 31st if the return is filed by a tax advisor. Freelancers have to apply for quarterly instalment payments at the *Finanzamt* when starting a business; these payments will be credited to your annual income tax and adjusted for future years based on the prior year. There is an annual tax-free exemption of €9,169 (as of 2019) and after that rates start at 14%, rising to 45%. If you earn above €17,500 a year, you will also need to charge VAT (19%).

Unlike full-time employees, in general, freelancers do not have to pay into the German social security system, i.e. governmental healthcare, unemployment and pension insurances. However, you will need to take out your own health insurance. This is mandatory and, unfortunately, will probably be quite expensive as you'll have to cover 100% of the cost.

Although you can do your taxes yourself, it's advisable to get a tax consultant, at least for your first year. Knowing that everything has been done correctly and that the *Finanzamt* won't be knocking on your door is worth the extra expense.

Do I have to submit a tax declaration?
People with very low income (under €9,000 per year) don't have to pay taxes and therefore don't need to fill out a tax declaration. Employees in tax brackets 1 (singles) and 4 (married people) are also not obliged to submit one. However, it is recommended because you will likely get some money back, especially during your first year in the country.

Do I need a tax consultant to do my tax declaration?
No, not necessarily. If your income situation is simple you might be able to handle it yourself. You can do your tax declaration online. But as soon as it gets more complicated (income from different sources / countries, children, etc.), it might be a good idea to seek professional help. Tax consultants can often provide tips and tricks. Having your tax declaration done by a professional in your first year in Germany is recommended because they will likely get a good amount of money back for various reasons (refund of relocation costs, income from different countries, etc.)

Useful vocabulary:

Taxes	Steuern
Tax office	Finanzamt
Tax declaration	Steuererklärung
Tax consultant	Steuerberater
Tax number	Steuernummer
Tax ID	Steueridentifikationsnummer / Steuer-ID
Tax bracket	Steuerklasse
Income tax (for employees)	Lohnsteuer
Income tax (for freelancers)	Einkommensteuer
Social security contribution	Sozialabgabe
Solidarity surcharge	Solidaritätsbeitrag
Church tax	Kirchensteuer
Health insurance	Krankenversicherung
Pension insurance	Rentenversicherung
Care insurance	Pflegeversicherung
Unemployment insurance	Arbeitslosenversicherung
VAT	Umsatzsteuer (outdated: Mehrwertsteuer)
Salary	Gehalt / Lohn
Net / gross	netto / brutto
Tax refund	Steuerrückzahlung
Renounce membership of a church	Kirchenaustritt
Registry office	Standesamt
District court	Amtsgericht
Catholic	katholisch
Protestant	evangelisch / protestantisch
Jewish	jüdisch
Muslim	muslimisch
Baptism	Taufe
Confirmation	Bescheinigung
Where's the tax office?	Wo ist das Finanzamt?
I'd like to change my tax bracket.	Ich möchte meine Steuerklasse wechseln.
When / how do I get my tax ID number?	Wann / wie bekomme ich meine Steueridentifikationsnummer?
Do I have to fill out a form?	Muss ich ein Formular ausfüllen?

Do you need any further information?	Brauchen Sie weitere Informationen?
I'd like to renounce my membership of the church.	Ich möchte aus der Kirche austreten.
I'd like to submit my tax declaration.	Ich möchte meine Steuererklärung einreichen.
I'm looking for a tax consultant.	Ich suche einen Steuerberater.
I have a tax consultant.	Ich habe einen Steuerberater.
Will I get a tax refund?	Bekomme ich eine Steuerrückzahlung?
When / how will I get the refund?	Wann / wie bekomme ich die Rückzahlung?
Can I do that online?	Kann ich das online machen?
Do I have to sign this?	Muss ich das unterschreiben?
Will I get this automatically?	Bekomme ich das automatisch?
Will this happen automatically?	Passiert das automatisch?

Test yourself
Taxes
Steuern

1. Wo ist das Finanzamt?

a. Wo wohnen Sie?
b. Im Zentrum.
c. Sie bekommen eine Rückzahlung.
d. Das Finanzamt ist am Montag geschlossen.

2. Ich möchte meine Steuerklasse wechseln?

a. Sind Sie verheiratet?
b. Es gibt sechs Steuerklassen.
c. Meine Tochter ist in der vierten Klasse.
d. Zusammen oder getrennt?

3. Wann bekomme ich meine Steuer-ID?

a. Im Winter in Hamburg
b. An der Ampel
c. Nächste Woche per Post
d. Gestern

4. Muss ich ein Formular ausfüllen?

a. Ja, aber Sie können es auch online machen.
b. Nein, Sie bekommen die Rückzahlung.
c. Haben Sie ein Formular?
d. Ist das Ihre Steuererklärung?

5. Brauchen Sie weitere Informationen?

a. Nein, Sie müssen unterschreiben.
b. Nein, das ist alles.
c. Das ist die Kirchensteuer.
d. Die Informationen finden Sie im Internet.

6. Bekomme ich das automatisch?

a. Ja, kein Problem.
b. Ja, mit der Post.
c. Nein, Sie bekommen keine Rückzahlung.
d. Nein, wir brauchen die Steuererklärung.

Answers: 1b, 2a, 3c, 4a, 5b, 6b

CHAPTER 8
Public transport
Öffentliche Verkehrsmittel

The German public transport system is (for the most part) pretty fantastic so unless you live or work in the middle of nowhere, public transport is easily the best way to get around. A weekly, monthly or yearly ticket will work out cheaper than buying single tickets for every trip but beware the bewildering ticket machines - make sure you're buying the right ticket for the right zone or time period. Most ticket machines have the option to switch language, which makes things a little easier.

Just in case you weren't confused enough, bear in mind that you can buy tickets on some forms of transport but not on others; some machines take cards and others don't so always have some cash handy, just in case.

Since the systems vary from city to city, here are some useful tips for getting around the four biggest cities in Germany:

BERLIN: You have to validate your ticket. This means that when your ticket pops out of the machine, you have to take it to another machine which stamps the time and date on it. Berlin, unlike other major capital cities, is based on a system of trust which is really rather lovely of the Berliners.

However, when the ticket inspectors do come, they come in force - and in plain clothes so you won't recognize them until the doors have already closed and it's too late. These guys have heard every excuse and nobody likes a *"Schwarzfahrer"* (fare dodger, or literally, "black rider" - brilliant German words). There's nothing quite like that cold, clammy sweat that breaks out when you realize you have a ticket but forgot to validate it...

Of course, there's always a chance that the inspectors will catch another *Schwarzfahrer* before they get to you. If this happens, on your marks, get set, go! Dash through the doors as the train arrives at the platform, spot the nearest validation machine, insert ticket, impatiently wait for click, race back to the train just as the doors are closing, dive through just in the nick of time before calmly retaking your seat, feeling a bit like

Indiana Jones. But unless you badly need more adventure in your life, buying and validating a ticket is probably easier.

You can do this on S-Bahn and U-Bahn platforms, on the bus and on the tram. You don't need exact change. The ticket is valid for 2 hours for the complete system; you can change from train to bus and back again as often as you like, but only in one direction.

HAMBURG: You do not have to validate your ticket. But that means that you can't buy a bunch of tickets in advance because they are only valid from the moment you buy them. You can switch and pause, but again only in one direction - no round trips.

MUNICH: Surprise, you have to validate your ticket again - although some machines do give you the option of pre-validating your ticket. The period of validity depends on the number of zones and varies from 1 to 4 hours. Again, no round trips.

COLOGNE: Brace yourself: tickets bought at the machines don't have to be validated, ones bought at ticket counters do. Depending on the price level, tickets can be valid from 20 minutes to 6 hours.

FAQ:

Do I need to validate my ticket every time I get on a different train / bus?
No, just validate your ticket once (if you have to) at the start of your journey and keep it with you for as long as the ticket is valid.

What's the cheapest ticket?
The single ticket (*Einzelfahrschein*) is usually quite expensive and only worth it if you're just taking one trip that day. Starting from two trips, the day ticket (*Tageskarte*) or weekly ticket (*Wochenkarte*) will probably work out cheaper. If you're traveling in a group, check out the group tickets (*Gruppenkarte*) or even group day tickets (*Gruppentageskarte*).

Where can I buy a monthly or yearly ticket?
Again, it depends on the city. You will always be able to buy them at service centers (but usually not at the standard ticket counters). Sometimes you can also get them online or at the machines.

How much is the fine for not having a valid ticket?

This can be quite expensive. In the four main cities, the fine for *Schwarzfahren* is €60. If they catch you three times, an official complaint will be filed and you'll get an even higher fine or, if you refuse to pay, you can be sent to jail - a slightly less orthodox way of finding a place to stay...

Can I get away with not paying fines?

If you're leaving the country and never planning on coming back, probably. If you're living here, unlikely - German bureaucracy will always find you.

Does public transport run during the night and on public holidays?

On weekends and public holidays, the trains and buses usually run all night. During the week, there will be a reduced bus service (that might replace the subway) between roughly 1 a.m. and 5 a.m. On weekends, the schedules are usually reduced during the day compared to weekdays, and public holidays have the same schedule as Sundays.

Can I bring my dog or bike with me?

Again, very different from city to city and can also be pretty complicated. In Munich for example, the dog is free but you have to buy a ticket for your bike. In Berlin, they charge you for both unless your small dog is in a "suitable container." Depending on your ticket, you may or may not be allowed to bring the dog free.

Please also bear in mind that in some cities there are certain times when you can't bring your bike (rush hour).

Expat story:
"Actual announcement I once heard on a train:
'Ladies and gentlemen, we regret that this train is running late and we will arrive at Göttingen approximately 30 minutes late. Connecting trains will not wait; any affected passengers are invited to speak to staff on this train who will be able to advise them of alternative connections. Click -- buzz -- click... Hang on, this is Göttingen! Uh... ladies and gentlemen, it appears we are, in fact, on time after all...'"
Rob, UK

Useful vocabulary:

Public transport	Öffentlicher Nahverkehr
Subway	U-Bahn
Local train	S-Bahn
Bus	Bus
Tram	Straßenbahn / Tram
Ticket	Ticket / Fahrkarte / Fahrschein
Single ticket	Einzelticket / Einzelfahrschein
Round-trip	Hin- und Rückfahrt
Extension ticket	Anschlussticket
Short trip	Kurzstrecke
Dog ticket	Hundeticket
Bicycle ticket	Fahrradticket
Validate	entwerten
subway / local train station	Station
Bus / tram stop	Haltestelle
train station	Bahnhof
Out of service	außer Betrieb
Please board.	Einsteigen bitte.
Please stand back.	Zurückbleiben bitte.
Mind the gap between platform and train.	Beachten Sie die Lücke zwischen Zug und Bahnsteigkante.
Tickets, please.	Die Fahrscheine, bitte.
This train terminates here. All change please.	Dieser Zug endet hier. Bitte alle aussteigen.
Exit right / left	Ausstieg rechts / links
Train arriving	Zug fährt ein / Zugeinfahrt
Train canceled	Zug fällt aus / Zugausfall
Delayed	Verspätet / Zugverspätung
I'd like to buy a ... ticket, please.	Ich hätte gern ein ....Ticket.
How much is the ticket?	Was kostet das Ticket?
I'll take...	Ich nehme....
Can I pay by card / credit card?	Kann ich mit Karte / Kreditkarte bezahlen?
Where is the bus stop?	Wo ist die Bushaltestelle?
How many stations to...?	Wie viele Stationen bis...?
Where does this train go to?	Wohin fährt dieser Zug?
Does this train / bus go to...?	Fährt dieser Zug / Bus nach...?
Does this train / bus stop at...?	Hält dieser Zug / Bus in...?
When does the train / bus arrive?	Wann kommt der Zug / Bus?
Can you help me, please?	Können Sie mir bitte helfen?
Can I get through?	Darf ich durch? / Darf ich vorbei?

Test yourself
Public transport
Öffentliche Verkehrsmittel

1. Ich hätte gern ein Einzelticket.

a. 2,60 Euro bitte
b. Wie heißen Sie?
c. Entschuldigung
d. Nicht so gut und Ihnen?

2. Wohin fährt dieser Zug?

a. Hamburg
b. 5 Euro
c. Nach Dresden
d. Ich komme aus Brasilien.

3. Wo ist die Bushaltestelle?

a. Die Tram?
b. Einsteigen bitte
c. Haben Sie eine Fahrkarte?
d. In der Hauptstraße

4. Können Sie mir helfen?

a. Wo ist die U-Bahn-Station?
b. Ja, natürlich
c. Wie geht's?
d. Es kostet 9 Euro.

5. Hin- und Rückfahrt?

a. Nein, nur Hinfahrt
b. Ein Hundeticket, bitte
c. Nach München
d. Guten Tag

6. Hält dieser Zug in Hamburg Hauptbahnhof?

a. In Berlin Hauptbahnhof
b. Nein, ich heiße Müller
c. Ja, gerne
d. Ja, der Zug hält in Hamburg Altona und Hauptbahnhof

Answers: 1a, 2c, 3d, 4b, 5a, 6d

CHAPTER 9
Directions
Wegbeschreibungen

Although Google Maps is an absolute life-saver, there may come a time when technology fails and you have to ask an actual human for help. And even Google has got nothing when it comes to roaming the labyrinthine corridors of the various *Ämter*...

Looking hopelessly lost won't help you - Germans usually won't say anything unless you approach them but, when you do, they'll probably do their best to give you a hand. Likewise, if someone asks you for directions, think how amazing it will be to be able to answer them in fluent (OK, passable) German!

Useful vocabulary:

Left	links
Right	rechts
Straight	geradeaus
North / South / East / West	Norden / Süden / Osten / Westen
Here	hier
There	da / dort
This way / that way	hier entlang / da entlang
Far	weit
In front of / behind	vor / hinter
Between / next to	zwischen / neben
Over / Under	über / unter
Close	nah / in der Nähe
Walk	gehen
Drive / Ride	fahren
Cross	überqueren
Turn	abbiegen
Street	Straße
Corner	Ecke
Intersection	Kreuzung
Roundabout	Kreisverkehr
Bridge	Brücke
Traffic Lights	Ampel

Pedestrian crossing / Crosswalk	Fußgängerüberweg / Fußgängerübergang / Zebrastreifen
Sidewalk	Bürgersteig / Gehweg
Bike path	Fahrradweg
Building	Gebäude
House	Haus
First / second door on the right / left	die erste / zweite Tür rechts / links
Up the stairs / down the stairs	oben / unten
On foot	zu Fuß
By bike / car / train	Mit dem Fahrrad / Auto / Zug
By subway / Tram	Mit der U-Bahn / Tram
Excuse me, can you help me?	Entschuldigung, können Sie mir helfen?
Are you from around here?	Sind Sie von hier?
Where is …?	Wo ist …?
I'm looking for…	Ich suche...
How do I find…?	Wie finde ich…?
Sorry, unfortunately I don't know that either.	Entschuldigung, das weiß ich leider auch nicht.
I'm lost.	Ich habe mich verlaufen.
Is it far?	Ist es weit?
It's (not) far from here.	Es ist (nicht) weit von hier.
It's close.	Es ist nah / in der Nähe.
How long will it take?	Wie lange dauert es?
It'll take about ten minutes.	Es dauert circa / ungefähr zehn Minuten.
Can I walk?	Kann ich zu Fuß gehen?
Go straight on Main Street.	Gehen Sie geradeaus die Hauptstraße entlang.
Turn right.	Biegen Sie rechts ab. / Gehen Sie nach rechts.
Turn left at the traffic lights.	Biegen Sie an der Ampel ab.
Take the subway.	Nehmen Sie die U-Bahn.
Take the elevator to the … floor.	Nehmen Sie den Aufzug / Fahrstuhl in den … Stock.
Go over the bridge and you'll see the building to your left.	Gehen Sie über die Brücke, dann sehen Sie das Gebäude links.

Test yourself
Directions
Wegbeschreibungen

1. Entschuldigung, sind Sie von hier?

a. Ja, ich komme aus Japan.
b. Nein, ich spreche Spanisch.
c. Nein, ich bin auch nur Tourist.
d. Ja, ich interessiere mich für die Wohnung.

2. Wo ist der Supermarkt?

a. Ich habe mich verlaufen.
b. Ich bin nicht von hier.
c. Eine Briefmarke bitte.
d. An der nächsten Kreuzung links.

3. Ist es weit?

a. Nein, es ist in der Nähe.
b. Stimmt so.
c. Ja, zusammen bitte.
d. Ich möchte meine Wohnung anmelden.

4. Wie lange dauert es?

a. An der Ampel
b. 10 Minuten
c. Circa 20 Euro
d. 100 Meter

5. Kann ich zu Fuß gehen?

a. Nein, nehmen Sie die U-Bahn.
b. Ja, kaufen Sie ein Ticket.
c. Nein, die Station ist in der Lindenstraße.
d. Ja, Sie können mit Karte bezahlen.

6. Wo ist die Post?

a. Per Einschreiben?
b. Ich möchte den Vertrag kündigen.
c. Was sind die Konditionen?
d. Das weiß ich leider auch nicht.

Answers: 1c, 2d, 3a, 4b, 5a, 6d

CHAPTER 10
Driving
Auto fahren

Driving in Germany is an absolute joy. Germans are just crazy about cars and, as you'll quickly realize, maybe a bit crazy in general. During your time here, you'll hear many Germans complaining about the low driving standards - it's kind of a national pastime. If you want to fit in, nod and grumble along with them, but really they don't know how good they have it. Compared to the cramped streets of Paris, the gridlocks of American metropolises or the scooter-clogged madness of Vietnam, German driving quality, safety levels and infrastructure are up there with the world's best.

But even in this drivers' paradise, there are a few things to keep in mind.

Of course everyone knows about the unrestricted speed limits on the *Autobahn* but, for speed-freaks and the speed-averse alike, there is one golden rule: Respect the Fast Lane. When old Granny Schmidt is dawdling along at 60 km/h in the middle lane and you're just itching to overtake her, it's go-go precision eyesight time; that tiny dot barely visible in your side-view mirror can quickly become a honking great beast of a Mercedes bearing down on you.

Likewise, if you fancy pushing the limits of your little old rental car in the fast lane and that dot appears again, head over to the slower lanes as quickly and safely as possible. Not only will you avoid the passive-aggressive glare of a German whose fuel efficiency statistics you've just ruined, you'll also be driving like a safe and respectable German motorist. And be aware that the majority of *Autobahnen* do have speed restrictions, at least for some parts, and that there are speed cameras along many of those stretches.

In the cities, there are two main things to remember. The first, which may or may not come as a surprise, is that the concept of an overtaking lane does not exist in urban areas - undertaking someone (passing by a car in the middle lane using the slow lane) is perfectly legal here as long as you obey the speed limit.

The second is to watch out for cyclists. Germany has an excellent cycling infrastructure, which becomes very obvious when you're turning right at a junction in a city. Even in normally sensible Germany, there are plenty of complete idiots who insist on riding around with no lights, so when the traffic light goes green, edge forward a meter or two and then wait until you are 100% sure the moment is right and the way is clear. Better to deal with a few impatient beeps than an angry dent in your side panel and an equally dented cyclist rolling around in the street. The "complete idiot" defence is not a thing here.

Expat story:

"When I first moved here, I went to a gas station to fill up. In the USA, you first *authorize a card at the pump, and only after that can you pump gas into your vehicle. Decades of conditioning my brain. So I go to a station, jet lagged, and begin pumping the German way (pump first, pay later). Once the pump clicks off, my Pavlov response kicks in and I jump into the car and drive away.*

A few months later I get a letter from a detective asking me to see her to discuss alleged petrol fraud. She is super serious and shows me video footage, and asks like it's straight from a movie, "Herr Riley, why did you do it??" Like there was some mysterious motive. So I explain how it is in the USA, how I had just arrived, and how it was a simple mistake.

She shakes her head and asks me to go to the gas station and settle with them otherwise she has to escalate to a higher authority.

I went back the station and settled up, casually stating "I bet this happens a lot with US citizens, eh?" Blank stare. She was like, "What, theft of motor fuel? No, I have never seen it before, it is a shocking thing."

I settled the amount, thanked her in German, and walked out feeling like the biggest loser of all time."

Matt, USA

FAQ:

Which foreign driver's licences are valid in Germany?
EU licences and those from the European Economic Area (Norway, Liechtenstein, Iceland) are valid without restrictions, others are limited.

How long is my foreign driving licence valid in Germany?
After moving to Germany, your (non-EU) licence is valid for 6 months. After that, you'll have to get a German licence. An extension of the 6-month period is possible if the licence holder can prove that they won't be staying in the country for more than 12 months.

How do I get a German licence?

Depending on your country of origin, there might be a special agreement and you won't have to take a driving exam, you can just exchange your old licence for the German one (bear in mind that you might have to hand in your old one and you won't get it back). You might have to take a practical test but not the theoretical one.

If there are no agreements between your country and Germany, you'll have to take both tests (theoretical and practical). You need to go to a driving school to register and the fee will be around €100.

If you don't have a foreign licence and want to get a German licence, you'll have to take the required classes at a driving school. Please note that these are quite expensive - the total fees for the classes plus the tests could add up to over €1,500.

Do I need an eye test or any other regular tests in order to get and keep my licence?

You have to do an eye test before you can sign up for the driving tests. You can do it at any optician, it's not very expensive and you don't need an appointment. You only have to do the test once - the result will either say "Needs glasses" or "Doesn't need glasses" and this will be written in your licence (and will stay there forever).

Before taking the driving test you will also have to attend a first-aid course. It's usually about 10 classes (often offered as a weekend course) and costs around €25 per person. There are various companies or institutions that offer them like, for example, the Red Cross.

After you've obtained your licence, you will never have to take any test again and you can legally drive even if you can barely move or see anymore.

What are the additional costs if I buy a car?

You'll have to pay taxes (*KFZ-Steuer*), which depend on the age, type of motor and capacity of the car. Roughly, you can calculate €100 to €300 per year for a midsize car.

Insurance (*KFZ-Versicherung*) is mandatory. The fee depends on many factors but €500 per year is a very rough estimate.

What do I need to register my car?

You'll have to go to the registration office (*Zulassungsbehörde*) - it's probably best to make an appointment - and bring along the following documents:

- Your passport
- Proof of insurance
- Two types of car ID documents that you received with the purchase of the vehicle (these are called *"Zulassungsbescheinigung Teil I & II"*, or formerly: *Fahrzeugschein* & *Fahrzeugbrief* (some people might still use the old names))
- Proof of inspection (*TÜV*, see below)

What is TÜV?

TÜV (Technischer Überwachungsverein) is the association for technical inspection of vehicles. Every motor vehicle has to get a general inspection every 24 to 36 months (depending on its age). You can only register your car, motorbike, etc. with a valid *TÜV*-seal (displayed on the licence plate). The inspection costs between €70 and €100. If you drive a car with an expired seal, you'll be fined.

Can I just park any old way?

No, this is Germany and *alles muss in Ordnung sein* (everything must be in order). You have to park in the direction of the traffic. There must be a gap of at least 3 meters between your vehicle and the middle of the street or the nearest lane separator. Signage for on-street parking may require you to use a voucher, disc, or meter to limit the length of time you can park. Parking fines generally range from €5 to €25 and, if you obstruct traffic or a driveway, your vehicle will almost certainly be towed. If this happens, you need to call the police to resolve the situation.

Is it possible to take the theoretical / practical test in English or other languages?

In the big cities, you can take the test and do the lessons in English and some other languages.

What if I'm in an accident?

If you're unlucky enough to be in an accident, there are certain procedures that must be followed. First of all, you need to stop immediately. The same rule applies if you're not involved in the accident but are a direct witness. If someone is injured, call for an ambulance and the police. You are required by law to give first aid to any injured people. If nobody is injured, and the vehicles can be moved safely, you should mark the location of each vehicle, then move them out of traffic. Secure the accident site using a warning triangle placed 100 meters behind the scene (200 meters on the *Autobahn*). It's a good idea to call the police to the scene even if nobody is injured so that you won't have problems with your insurance company down the line. If you damage an unoccupied vehicle, you are required to wait at the scene for 30 minutes for the owner to return. If the owner does not return, you must then report the accident to the police. Once the police have cleared you, you're free to go.

Is there really no speed limit in Germany?
There are speed limits for most streets, in the city (usually 50 km/h, or 30 km/h in residential areas or near schools) or connecting cities (usually 100 km/h). But sections of the famous *Autobahn* (highway) have no speed limit if not otherwise specified. If there's construction work or an accident, there will be signs.

Will the word "Fahrt" ever get unfunny?
No. (Snigger.)

Useful vocabulary:

Vehicle	Fahrzeug
Motor Vehicle	KFZ (Kraftfahrzeug)
Car	Auto / Wagen / PKW (Personenkraftwagen)
Truck	LKW (Lastkraftwagen) / Laster
Motorbike	Motorrad
Scooter	Roller
Bike	Fahrrad
Trailer	Anhänger
Camper van	Wohnmobil / Wohnwagen
Helmet	Helm
Driving licence	Führerschein
Registration office	Zulassungsbehörde
Vehicle registration paper	Zulassungsbescheinigung
Drive / ride	fahren
Driving school	Fahrschule
Driving lesson	Fahrstunde
Driving instructor	Fahrlehrer
Driving exam	Fahrprüfung
Theoretical / practical	theoretisch / praktisch
First-aid class	Erste-Hilfe-Kurs
Eye test	Sehtest / Augentest
Optician	Optiker
Street	Straße
Bike path	Fahrradweg
Highway	Autobahn
Street sign	Verkehrszeichen / Straßenschild
Traffic	Verkehr
Speed limit	Geschwindigkeitsbegrenzung
Speed control	Geschwindigkeitskontrolle
Speed camera	Blitzer
Parking ticket	Strafzettel
Traffic light	Ampel
Intersection	Kreuzung
Roundabout	Kreisverkehr
Technical Inspection of Vehicles Association	TÜV (Technischer Überwachungsverein)
Vehicle tax	Fahrzeugsteuer
Car insurance	KFZ-Versicherung / Autoversicherung
Fully comprehensive insurance	Vollkasko-Versicherung

Partially comprehensive insurance	Teilkasko-Versicherung
Accident	Unfall
Car keys	Autoschlüssel
Motor	Motor
Steering wheel	Steuer(rad)
Trunk	Kofferraum
Tyre	Reifen
Licence plate	Nummernschild
Gas station	Tankstelle
Refuel	tanken
Petrol	Benzin
I have a driving licence from...	Ich habe einen Führerschein aus...
Is it (the licence) valid?	Ist er gültig?
How long is it valid?	Wie lange ist er gültig?
I'd like to get my driving licence.	Ich möchte meinen Führerschein machen.
I'd like to take the eye test for the driving licence.	Ich möchte den Sehtest für den Führerschein machen.
Do I need to take a test / an exam?	Muss ich einen Test / eine Prüfung machen?
Where can I do that?	Wo kann ich das machen?
How much is the test?	Was kostet der Test?
How much does a driving lesson cost?	Was kostet eine Fahrstunde?
How many driving lessons do I have to take?	Wie viele Fahrstunden muss ich machen?
Do you offer driving lessons in English?	Bieten Sie Fahrstunden auf Englisch an?
Will the test be in English?	Ist der Test auf Englisch?
I have a car / no car.	Ich habe ein Auto / kein Auto.
I'd like to register my motorbike.	Ich möchte mein Motorrad anmelden.
How much is the tax?	Wie hoch sind die Steuern?
I'd like to sign up for car insurance.	Ich möchte eine Autoversicherung abschließen.
Driving licence and vehicle registration, please!	Führerschein und Fahrzeugschein bitte!
Please ride on the bike path.	Bitte fahren Sie auf dem Fahrradweg.

Test yourself
Driving
Auto fahren

1. Haben Sie einen Führerschein?

a. Ja, an der Ampel links.
b. Ja, aber aus Südafrika.
c. Nein, ich habe einen Sehtest.
d. Nein, wo ist die Kreuzung?

2. Ist mein Führerschein in Deutschland gültig?

a. Aus Belgien?
b. Stimmt so.
c. Ja, sechs Monate.
d. Nein, getrennt bitte.

3. Muss ich eine Prüfung machen?

a. Ja, den Erste-Hilfe-Kurs.
b. Es kostet 25 Euro.
c. Bitte fahren Sie mit Helm.
d. Ja, praktisch und theoretisch.

4. Ich möchte mein Auto anmelden.

a. Haben Sie alle Papiere?
b. Natürlich, ohne Nebenkosten.
c. Sind die Kurse auf Englisch?
d. Haben Sie Kinder?

5. Wie hoch sind die Steuern?

a. Nein, ich habe kein Auto.
b. 95 Euro im Jahr.
c. Monatlich.
d. Im Finanzamt.

6. Entschuldigung, ist das ein Strafzettel?

a. Ja, Sie können hier nicht parken.
b. Ja, das Auto ist grün.
c. Ja, Sie fahren auf dem Fahrradweg.
d. Ja, Sie fahren mit Helm.

Answers: 1b, 2c, 3d, 4a, 5b, 6a

CHAPTER 11
<u>Recycling</u>
Mülltrennung

By now, you've probably noticed the many colorful bins that reside in your courtyard - usually enough of them to strike fear and confusion into the heart of every newcomer to this fair land. You may even have heard "horror" stories about having to separate the teabag, staple, tag and string before disposing of them. Finding a sad-looking German friend in your kitchen holding up something you proudly thought you'd binned correctly is a rite of passage - and actually pretty funny.

But to the Germans, waste separation (*Mülltrennung*) is no laughing matter and, as a foreigner, chances are it'll take a while before you get the hang of it. In fact, you've probably already made some rookie mistakes. For example, baking paper, even though it's got paper in the name, does not go in the paper bin. And if that's not odd enough, a lot of Germans can't even agree on what goes where.

Don't, however, think that you can just not bother. Aside from the environmental benefits, many buildings seem to come with a busybody who makes it their life's work to go through the bins (yes, really) ensuring everything is *in Ordnung* - a very important German expression. Failure to take waste separation seriously can result in fines for the building, which will definitely not put you at the top of your new neighbors' Christmas card lists - and yes, they will know it's the foreigner. So, sit back with a nice cup of tea and learn how to *trenn* that *Müll* like a pro. OK, maybe forget the tea...

<u>FAQ:</u>

What goes where?
This sounds like a simple enough question but well, nothing in Germany is that simple. As a general rule:

Bio: for food / organic waste, e.g. vegetable and fruit peel, eggshells, coffee grounds, tea filters, food leftovers. It's a good idea to buy the compostable green bags that are available at every supermarket. You really don't want to see the inside of an emptied plastic bag that's had bio waste in it.

Verpackung: for lightweight packaging that isn't cardboard
Restmüll: all non-recyclable waste e.g. cigarette butts, diapers
Papier / Pappe: for waste paper e.g. newspapers, magazines, cardboard packaging (but not pizza boxes with bits of cheese stuck to them), unused napkins but not used ones...

For glass bottles and jars: green in *Grün*, brown in *Braun*, clear in *Weiß*. Often green and brown glass goes in the same bin ("*Buntglas*" - colored glass). Just be careful that you don't decide to throw away all of your glass bottles at night or on a Sunday or public holiday - there are quite strict noise laws in Germany and breaking them will not make you popular. But it could be worse - you could be living in Switzerland where someone might call the police on you for vacuuming on a Sunday. Lovely, lenient Germans...

What is the "*Pfand*" system and how does it work?
When you buy a soft drink or beer (bottle or can), most of the time there's a *Pfand* (deposit) included in the price. This ranges from 8 to 25 cents, which is written on the label. When you're done, bring these bottles and cans back to the store and pop them into the special machine - you'll get a receipt which will be deducted from your bill or paid out in cash at the register. There is no *Pfand* on wine bottles - they go in the normal glass bins. But remember, not on Sundays, public holidays or at night... and definitely not in Switzerland. If you're too lazy to return your bottles by yourself you can put them next to trash cans on the street. Homeless or poor people will pick them up to get the deposit. *Flaschensammeln* (collecting bottles) is very common among them for some extra change.

What do I do with old clothes and shoes?
Donate them to a second-hand store or drop them into the clothing bins you'll find dotted all over every part of Germany.

Which bin do batteries go in?
Most grocery stores, and also shops like Rossmann and DM, have a bin for old batteries, which is usually located close to the door.

What do I do with bulky waste?
Bulky waste that you can't transport yourself has to be picked up. You need to call the *Sperrmüll*, arrange a date for the pick-up and pay for it (prices start at about €10 depending on the amount of trash and how urgently you need it picked up). If you can transport your waste yourself, the cheaper option is to take it to a recycling center. These are usually

free and you should be able to find your nearest one pretty easily. (You'll find a link at the back of the book.)

Is it OK to leave stuff I don't want any more on the street?
No, though a lot of people do it. The truth is that sticking "*Geschenk*" on your clapped-out printer or collapsed, dog-eaten sofa does not make it a "gift." If your waste (furniture, kitchen appliances) is still useable somebody might pick it up. But instead of leaving your old mattress out in the rain, why not put up a poster of the stuff you want to get rid of or, even better, place an ad on eBay Kleinanzeigen (classifieds) - some people manage to clear out / furnish their entire apartments through this site. One man's trash is another man's treasure.

What do I do with my old Christmas tree?
This you can leave on the side of the street - there's a special pick-up day for Christmas trees.

Useful vocabulary:

Waste separation	Mülltrennung
General waste	Restmüll
Packaging waste	Verpackungsmüll
Plastic waste	Plastikmüll
Organic / food waste	Biomüll
Paper / cardboard	Papier / Pappe
Bulky waste	Sperrmüll
Green glass	Grünglas
Brown glass	Braunglas
Clear glass	Weißglas
Bottle	Flasche
Can	Dose
Throw away	wegwerfen
Deposit (for cans and bottles)	Pfand
waste collection	Müllabfuhr
How do I separate the waste?	Wie trenne ich den Müll?
Excuse me, which bin does this go in?	Entschuldigung, in welche Tonne kommt das?
Where's the nearest clothing bin?	Wo ist die nächste Altkleider-Sammlung?

Test yourself
Recycling
Mülltrennung

1. Entschuldigung, in welche Tonne kommt das?

a. In die Papiermülltonne.
b. Haben Sie ein Einkommen?
c. Bitte füllen Sie das Formular aus.
d. Mülltrennung.

2. Ist das Restmüll?

a. Ja, gerne.
b. 100 Euro pro Monat
c. Nein, das ist Plastikmüll.
d. Nein, danke.

3. Hat diese Flasche Pfand?

a. Ja, in 5 Minuten.
b. Die Nebenkosten sind inklusive.
c. Das kostet 25 Cent.
d. Ja, 25 Cent

4. Wo ist der Glas-Container?

a. Mit Pfand?
b. Der Container für Plastikmüll?
c. In der Hauptstraße.
d. Dosen haben auch Pfand.

5. Wann kommt die Müllabfuhr?

a. Es kostet 10 Euro!
b. Jeden Donnerstag
c. Mit dem Bus.
d. In der Hauptstraße.

6. Ist Sperrmüll kostenlos?

a. Im Recycling-Center ja.
b. Das ist Biomüll.
c. Haben Sie Mülltrennung in Spanien?
d. Nein, es hat kein Pfand.

Answers: 1a, 2c, 3d, 4c, 5b, 6a

CHAPTER 12
In a restaurant / bar / café
In einem Restaurant / einer Bar / einem Café

If you thought the Germans were quite a humorless, severe lot, just stroll past any café or restaurant with outdoor seating on those first sunny days of spring. Even though it's only around 8 degrees, every table will be packed with jolly Germans, talking and laughing, enjoying their *Kaffee und Kuchen*, a refreshing Aperol Spritz or a cheeky beer - all while wearing their sensible all-weather clothing, of course.

Eating out is a national pastime in Germany and you'll certainly never go hungry with the variety of places to choose from. And, even though the Germans might not be as renowned for their cuisine as, say, the French or the Italians, don't write them off just yet. Sure, maybe the first time you see raw minced meat topped with raw onions on bread, you might be tempted to flee the country but, chances are, you'll grow to love it. (Or maybe more realistically, after a few years, your stomach won't flip flop at the sight of it. Maybe.)

Portions here are humongous, so it's lucky the people are an active bunch or they probably would be too. There are around 600 different types of bread for you to munch your way through and, wait for it, an estimated 1,500 varieties of sausage.

Yes, in Germany, the sausage is king and, aside from just being eaten, it also enters the language in rather amusing ways. The next time you're out with your German friends, pause a little for dramatic effect and then hit them with "*Alles hat ein Ende nur die Wurst hat zwei*" - (Everything has an end, only the sausage has two), "*Du arme Wurst*" (You poor sausage = thing) or "*Es geht um die Wurst*" (It's about the sausage = It's do or die). Sit back and savor the fact that everyone now thinks you're rather a profound individual.

FAQ:

Can I pay by card?
It's better not to take the chance. A lot of places do accept card payments nowadays but smaller cafés and bars probably won't. Always have some cash handy, just in case.

Is it possible to pay separately?
Absolutely - you'll almost always be asked "together or separately?" (*zusammen oder getrennt?*) wherever you go.

Do I pay for each drink or can I start a tab?
It's far more common in Germany to pay at the end rather than after each drink.

How much should I tip?
About 10% is standard but it's very common to round the price up (€8.50 becomes €9, for example). Waiters are paid a (decent) wage here; they don't live entirely off their tips.

What's the service like in German bars and restaurants?
You won't find the hyper-friendly service that's common in the US, that's for sure. "Hi, my name's Gunther (big smile) and I'll be your server this evening (big smile)" doesn't really go with the German approach to customer service. But, for the most part, service is pleasant and efficient - just don't expect your waiter to be your new best friend.

Can I smoke in German bars?
This varies from state to state. Some states, like Bavaria, have an outright smoking ban. Some, like Berlin, are a lot more lax - you'll find *Raucherkneipen* (smoking pubs) on pretty much every corner but you have to be over 18 to enter. (See the list of smoking laws by state at the back of the book.)

Useful vocabulary:

Eat / drink	essen / trinken
Food / drinks	Essen / Getränke
Order (verb)	bestellen
Breakfast	Frühstück
Lunch	Mittagessen
Dinner	Abendessen
Menu	Speisekarte
Wine list	Weinkarte
Starters	Vorspeisen
Main courses	Hauptspeisen
Desserts	Nachtisch / Desserts
Meat dishes	Fleischgerichte
Beef	Rindfleisch
Steak (rare / medium / well-done)	Steak (blutig / halb durch / durch)
Lamb	Lamm
Pork	Schwein
Game	Wild
Poultry dishes	Geflügelgerichte
Chicken	Hühnchen / Hähnchen / Huhn
Turkey	Truthahn / Pute
Duck	Ente
Goose	Gans
Fish dishes	Fischgerichte
Salmon	Lachs
Trout	Forelle
Cod	Dorsch, Kabeljau
Herring	Hering
Sides	Beilagen
with potatoes / rice / noodles	mit Kartoffeln / Reis / Nudeln
Cake	Kuchen
Salt / pepper	Salz / Pfeffer
Mustard / ketchup	Senf / Ketchup
Oil / vinegar	Öl / Essig
Sugar	Zucker
Non-alcoholic drinks	nicht-alkoholische Getränke
Tea	Tee
Coffee	Kaffee
Juice	Saft
Red / white / rosé wine	Rotwein, Weißwein, Rosé
Dry / sweet (for wine)	trocken / lieblich
Light / dark beer	hell / dunkel

Draft beer	Fassbier
Still / sparkling water	Stilles Wasser / Sprudel
Carbonated	mit Kohlensäure
Milk	Milch
Cutlery	Besteck
Knife	Messer
Fork	Gabel
Spoon	Löffel
Cup	Tasse
Glass	Glas
Plate	Teller
Bowl	Schüssel
Pan	Pfanne
Napkin / serviette	Serviette
For here / to take away	für hier / zum Mitnehmen
Tip	Trinkgeld
Waiter / Waitress	Kellner / Kellnerin
Open / closed	geöffnet / geschlossen
Opening hours	Öffnungszeiten
A table for two, please.	Einen Tisch für zwei, bitte.
We have a reservation.	Wir haben reserviert.
Can I see a menu?	Kann ich die Speisekarte sehen?
Can I have the wine list?	Kann ich die Weinkarte haben?
Can I get an ashtray, please?	Kann ich bitte einen Aschenbecher bekommen?
I'm (just / still) waiting for someone.	Ich warte (nur / noch) auf jemanden.
Do you have any vegetarian / vegan options?	Haben Sie vegetarische / vegane Optionen?
Would you like to order?	Möchten Sie bestellen?
I'd / we'd like to order.	Ich / wir möchten bestellen.
I'm / we're ready.	Ich bin / wir sind fertig.
I'll have ... , please.	Ich möchte...., bitte.
I'll take....	Ich nehme....
Is it very spicy?	Ist es sehr scharf?
Can I have it with / without...	Kann ich es bitte mit / ohne ... haben?
Does it come with anything?	Gibt es etwas dazu?
Anything else?	Noch etwas?
That's all.	Das ist alles.
Bon appetit / Enjoy your meal.	Guten Appetit.

Can we have the check, please?	Können wir bitte die Rechnung haben? / Die Rechnung bitte.
Can I pay, please?	Kann ich bezahlen? / Bezahlen bitte.
I'd / we'd like to pay.	Ich möchte / wir möchten bezahlen.
Would you like to pay by card or cash?	Möchten Sie mit Karte oder bar bezahlen?
(Would you like to pay) together or separately?	Zusammen oder getrennt?
That'll be 9 euros.	Das macht 9 Euro.
Keep the change.	Stimmt so. / Der Rest ist für Sie.

Test yourself
In a restaurant / bar / café
In einem Restaurant / einer Bar / einem Café

1. Möchten Sie bestellen?

a. Nein, ich warte noch auf jemanden.
b. Mit Salz und Pfeffer?
c. Kann ich die Speisekarte haben?
d. Wo ist die Toilette?

2. Haben Sie vegetarische Optionen?

a. Möchten Sie ein Bier?
b. Nein, am Montag haben wir geschlossen.
c. Ja, wir haben eine Gemüsepfanne.
d. Ja, das Schnitzel kostet 8,90 Euro.

3. Eine Pizza bitte.

a. Mit Kartoffeln?
b. Für hier oder zum Mitnehmen?
c. Stimmt so.
d. Möchten Sie bestellen?

4. Kann ich den Salat bitte ohne Dressing haben?

a. Nein danke.
b. Heute nicht.
c. Natürlich gerne.
d. 3 Euro bitte.

5. Noch etwas?

a. Der Rest ist für Sie.
b. Ist die Pizza mit Salami?
c. Ich möchte bestellen.
d. Danke, das ist alles.

6. Das macht 8,90 Euro.

a. Zusammen oder getrennt?
b. Kann ich bitte die Weinkarte haben?
c. Stimmt so.
d. Mit Kohlensäure

Answers: 1a, 2c, 3b, 4c, 5d, 6c

CHAPTER 13
<u>Shopping</u>
Einkaufen

You may have heard that German cashiers are fast but nothing truly prepares you for the reality. There seems to be an unwritten law in Germany that states: "The cheaper the supermarket, the faster the cashiers," and you'll experience it for yourself the first time you visit a Lidl or Aldi. "Oh, come on. How fast can they be?" you scoff. "I've got this..."

Ha.

Beep, beep, beep, beep, beep - the cashier's hands are a blur as your items land unceremoniously on the tiny metal ledge in front of you. However ready you thought you were, you break out in a sweat as the panic kicks in. The items are mounting up and you just can't seem to get them into your bag quickly enough.

You start flinging things in there, forgetting that bread should be at the top and instead crushing it with a liter of milk and a bag of potatoes. The beeping stops, the cashier dubiously eyes your red face. She's done and you're not even halfway there. The frantic search for your wallet begins, the line lengthens behind you... welcome to the joys of grocery shopping in Germany!

<u>FAQ:</u>

What are the cheapest supermarkets?
The two cheapest chains are Aldi and Lidl and you can find them all over the country (Aldi is divided into North and South but they're basically the same). There are also other pretty cheap ones like Penny and Netto.

Where can I find organic products?
Nowadays every supermarket, even the cheapest ones, has a wide range of organic products. There are also dedicated, more expensive stores called "*Biomarkt*" or "*Bioladen*" that only carry organic products.

Do all supermarkets accept cards?
They accept German debit cards but maybe not credit cards. Most shops have a sign on the door which shows which cards they take so be sure to check. Then again, having to decide between eating that evening or buying toilet roll while you rummage apologetically for change is probably not a mistake you'll make twice.

Are shops open seven days a week?
Nope. Germans value their work-life balance and Sunday is considered a quiet day (*Ruhetag*). All supermarkets are closed, as are shopping malls. If you're really desperate, there may be some smaller shops open in the bigger cities - and supermarkets in the major train stations if you want to spend your Sunday in queues even longer than at the *Bürgeramt* - and you'll always find a gas station for the bare essentials.
You might end up cursing Sundays your first few weekends here as you open your fridge and find one, sad, out-of-date egg there, but chances are you'll come to appreciate them over time. Instead of traipsing around shopping malls for hours on end, looking at or buying stuff they don't need, the Germans would prefer to be out and about - on their bikes, walking their dogs, spending time with family and friends, eating and most likely drinking. Once you get used to it, it's really rather nice.

Useful vocabulary:

Supermarket	Supermarkt
Market	Markt
Shop	Laden
Open	offen / geöffnet
Closed	geschlossen
Opening hours	Öffnungszeiten
Push / pull	drücken / ziehen
Entrance / exit	Eingang / Ausgang
Section	Abteilung
Fruit	Obst
Vegetables	Gemüse
Meat	Fleisch
Bread	Brot
Dairy products	Milchprodukte
Frozen products	Gefrierprodukte
Household products	Haushaltsprodukte
Shop assistant	Verkäufer (male) / Verkäuferin (female)
Cashier	Kassierer (male) / Kassiererin (female)
Cash register	Kasse
Shopping cart / basket	Einkaufswagen / Einkaufskorb
Cash register closed	Kasse geschlossen
Pay	bezahlen
Change (money)	Wechselgeld / Kleingeld
Bag (cloth)	Tasche
Bag (plastic)	Tüte
Excuse me, where are the shopping baskets?	Entschuldigung, wo sind die Einkaufskörbe?
Do you have…?	Haben Sie…?
I'm looking for the …	Ich suche…
Where is the… section?	Wo ist die … Abteilung?
Would you like a bag?	Möchten Sie eine Tüte?
Can I have a bag, please?	Kann ich bitte eine Tüte haben?
Can I get a receipt?	Kann ich bitte den Beleg / Kassenbon / Bon / Kassenzettel haben?
I'd like to pay by card.	Ich möchte mit Karte bezahlen

I'm sorry, I gave you a twenty / fifty.	Entschuldigung, ich habe Ihnen einen Zwanziger / Fünfziger gegeben.
Two euros back (change).	Zwei Euro zurück.
Have a nice day.	Schönen Tag.
Have a nice evening.	Schönen Abend.
Have a nice weekend.	Schönes Wochenende.
You too / same to you.	Gleichfalls, ebenfalls, ebenso, auch so (both formal and informal)
	Ihnen auch! (formal)
	Dir auch! (informal)

Test yourself
Shopping
Einkaufen

1. Entschuldigung, wo sind die Einkaufswagen?

a. Möchten Sie eine Tüte?
b. Links neben der Tür.
c. Stimmt so.
d. Ja, der Eingang ist hier.

2. Haben Sie Produkte aus Frankreich?

a. Sprechen Sie Französisch?
b. Nein, ich komme nicht aus Frankreich.
c. Nein, leider nicht.
d. Ja, mit Karte bitte.

3. Kann ich bitte den Kassenzettel haben?

a. Natürlich, gerne.
b. Nein, es ist geschlossen.
c. Ja, zusammen bitte.
d. An der Kasse links.

4. 10 Euro zurück.

a. Entschuldigung, aber ich habe Ihnen einen Fünfziger gegeben!
b. Gleichfalls.
c. Der Laden ist geöffnet.
d. 50 Cent, danke.

5. Möchten Sie eine Tüte?

a. Nein, ich nehme die U-Bahn.
b. Nein danke, ich habe eine Tasche.
c. Ja, Obst bitte.
d. Nein, das ist alles.

6. Schönen Abend!

a. Guten Tag.
b. Ich möchte mit Karte bezahlen.
c. Heute Abend.
d. Danke, ebenso.

Answers: 1b, 2c, 3a, 4a, 5b, 6d

CHAPTER 14
<u>Children</u>
Kinder

Being a kid in Germany looks like the most fun ever. Life here is active and outdoorsy. A *Laufrad* (training bike) is pretty much a rite of passage, and playgrounds are absolutely everywhere. German kids are pretty confident, probably due to the slightly more hands-off style of parenting here, so don't be overly surprised if a random child starts up a conversation with you in a café or on public transport. You can also be prepared for the bemused look you'll get because of your "funny" German. However, for parents, there are obviously quite a few practical considerations, some of which are dealt with here.

For a bit of background, it took German lawmakers quite a while to realize that the traditional family (the father as the breadwinner while the mother stays home to take care of the kids) was outdated and that the new family model could also mean single parents, working mums in high-paid jobs, patchwork families, same-sex-partnerships, and so on. A better childcare system was desperately needed, as well as good financial support for parents so they could stop working in order to have, and care for, a child. New and useful laws like income-based parental allowance, strict regulations regarding parental leave, and free childcare in some regions have since been introduced, making Germany a much more supportive environment in which to start a family.

<u>FAQ:</u>

Will I get financial support for my children?
Every parent living in Germany, regardless of their nationality or income, will receive a monthly sum for each child, the "*Kindergeld*". As of 2019, the *Kindergeld* is €194 for each of the first two children, increasing for additional kids. The parents receive *Kindergeld* until the child reaches 18 years of age. After that, it's possible to apply for an extension until the child reaches the age of 25 if the child is still in school (vocational training) or university.

Will I receive the *Kindergeld* automatically?
No, you have to apply for it (you'll find the link to the forms at the back of the book).

Is the *Kindergeld* the only financial support?

No, the mother receives a small amount a few weeks before and after the birth called "*Mutterschaftsgeld*" (motherhood money). From this day on, the parent taking care of the child is also entitled to "*Elterngeld*" (parental allowance) which is about 65% of their previous income or a maximum of €1,800 per month. Parents can apply for Elterngeld for up to 14 months (but 12 months maximum for one parent).

Will I lose my job if I take parental leave?

No, by law, your company cannot fire you during your "*Elternzeit*" (parental leave). Just make sure to tell HR how long you'll be gone for before you leave. *Elternzeit* can be up to 3 years but make sure to talk about it in detail with your employer.

Is childcare free in Germany?

It depends on the state you live in. Some states have free childcare from age 1, others only from age 3 or 5. If you do have to pay for it, don't forget that you can deduct it from your taxes.

How do I find a *Kita*?

In some areas (for example, Berlin), it can be very difficult to find a spot so make sure you start looking as early as possible - even during the pregnancy! It is a good idea to visit *Kitas* near you and let them know when you'd like your child to start (even if it's going to be two years later - no joke). This way they can plan ahead and save a place for you.

Is it compulsory to attend *Kita* and school?

Parents are not obliged to send their children to *Kita*, however more than 90% of 3- to 6-year-olds attend. School on the other hand is not voluntary - homeschooling is illegal in Germany. Children must attend school from 6 to 18 years old or until they finish their vocational training.

When do children start *Kita* and school?

It's up to the parents when their kids start Kita. 3 years old used to be the standard but, with more and more mothers working, it's become common to start as early as one year old. Childcare options for babies younger than that are difficult to find.

Children start school at 6 years of age. A test is carried out to make sure the child's development is sufficient; if not, school can be delayed for a year.

What do schools cost?
There are private schools but the quality of public schools is fine and the vast majority of children go there. Public schools are free.

What are the school hours?
Depending on the state and even the school, the lessons might end in the early- or mid-afternoon. Many schools also offer after-school programs if the parents have to work late.

Useful vocabulary:

Child, children	Kind, Kinder
Baby	Baby
Toddler	Kleinkind
Mother, father, parents	Mutter, Vater, Eltern
Parent (only one person)	Elternteil
Son, daughter	Sohn, Tochter
Birth	Geburt
Raise / bring up	erziehen
Single-parent	alleinerziehend (Adjektiv)
Look after	betreuen
Kindergarten	Kindergarten / Kita
Kindergarten teacher	Erzieher (male) / Erzieherin (female)
Play	spielen
Sleep	schlafen
Eat	essen
Paint	malen
Handicraft	basteln
Toys	Spielzeug
Inside / outside	drinnen / draußen
Playground	Spielplatz
School	Schule
Teacher	Lehrer (male) / Lehrerin (female)
Lesson	Unterricht
School subject	Schulfach
Maths	Mathe
German	Deutsch
Biology	Biologie
Chemistry	Chemie
Physics	Physik
History	Geschichte
Language	Sprache
P.E.	Sport
Book	Buch
Notebook	Heft
Pen	Stift
Grade	Note
Notepaper	Zeugnis
Holidays	Ferien

I'd like to apply for children's allowance.	Ich möchte Kindergeld beantragen.
My child was born on…	Mein Kind wurde am… geboren.
My son / daughter is … years old.	Mein Sohn / meine Tochter ist … Jahre alt.
I'd like to take 12 months of parental leave.	Ich möchte 12 Monate Elternzeit nehmen.
Is this Kita free?	Ist diese Kita kostenlos?
Are there any vacancies?	Gibt es freie Plätze?
I'd like to register my child.	Ich möchte mein Kind anmelden.

Test yourself
Children
Kinder

1. Haben Sie Kinder?

a. Die Rechnung bitte.
b. Nein, das ist alles.
c. Ja, aber sie sind in Korea.
d. Ja, mit Milch bitte.

2. Wie alt ist Ihr Kind?

a. Mein Hund ist acht.
b. Meine Tochter ist sieben.
c. Meine Wohnung ist in der Nähe.
d. Mein Auto ist alt.

3. Ich möchte Kindergeld beantragen.

a. Für zwei Kinder?
b. 100 Euro?
c. Zusammen oder getrennt?
d. Wo ist die Schule?

4. Wann wurde Ihr Sohn geboren?

a. In drei Tagen
b. 10 Minuten
c. In Pakistan
d. Im Dezember 2010

5. Sind Sie alleinerziehend?

a. Ja, ich habe ein Auto.
b. Nein, ich wohne nicht in Deutschland.
c. Nein, meine Frau wohnt auch hier.
d. Ja, ich habe zwei Kinder.

6. Ich möchte die Lehrerin sprechen.

a. Natürlich, wann haben Sie Zeit?
b. In Mathe?
c. Die Ferien sind im Sommer.
d. Haben Sie Elternzeit?

Answers: 1c, 2b, 3a, 4d, 5c, 6a

CHAPTER 15
Making and canceling contracts
Verträge abschließen und kündigen

Dealing with contracts in your native language can be tricky enough, but when facing German legalese, there's a fair chance your brain will turn to mush. German contracts are notoriously awful and getting out of them early usually requires leaving the country or faking your own death.

Unfortunately, contracts are pretty much unavoidable if you want to live like a real grown-up. Getting a job, an apartment, WiFi in said apartment, a phone, taking out insurance, joining a gym - all require your signature on that dotted line. It goes without saying that you should read every contract thoroughly and understand everything before signing it. If you're working at an international / English-speaking company, you may be given a "courtesy contract" in English. However, rental, phone, internet and gym contracts will most likely be in German, with the "*gut zu wissen*" (good to know) section tucked way in the back in tiny writing. It's probably a good idea to get a (very) patient German friend to go through any contracts with you before signing but, just in case you don't have any yet, here's some useful information to get you started.

FAQ:

What should I look out for?

RENTAL CONTRACT: Most importantly, check if the notice period in the contract is what you've agreed on with the landlord or agency. If it's a permanent rental, the legal period should be 3 months. Often landlords add other clauses though, especially with foreigners. *Zeitmietverträge* (temporary rental agreements) end automatically after a certain time.

Are the rent and the additional costs (*Nebenkosten*) exactly what you expected? Look out for *Staffelmiete* - this means that the rent will automatically go up after a few months or a year. Also note that the landlord can only charge you the *Nebenkosten* that are stated in the contract - no surprise charges!

Check if it says anything about renovation when moving out (you're often obliged to repaint the walls), the deposit (legally not higher than three months' cold rent), the conditions of the deposit, if you're allowed to keep pets, etc.

EMPLOYMENT CONTRACT: The notice period can be vary extensively, anything from one month to the end of the next quarter. Also check how long your trial period (*Probezeit*) will be and what the conditions are during this time, for example, can you take a vacation? Other important facts: Your salary including bonus payments (for example, some companies give a Christmas bonus), conditions for overtime (paid?), amount of vacation days (legally a minimum of 20 days if you're working full-time and do a 5-day week), can you work from home, other benefits (language classes, gym membership, transport, company phone or car), conditions for sick leave (after how many days do you have to hand in a doctor's certificate?), etc.

PHONE / MOBILE PHONE CONTRACT: Be very careful here because phone contracts have long notice periods (usually 3 months, but sometimes up to one year before the expiry date). For internet and landlines, check when the company will start providing the service - it's been known to take an eternity, often longer than 4 weeks. Also, before choosing one mobile phone company over another, check online how their reception in your area is. This can vary widely and you don't want to end up with a mobile phone that doesn't work where you live. (There are links for some of the major providers at the back of the book.)

If you want to cancel any type of phone contract, make sure you do it by registered mail (*per Einschreiben*). Otherwise the company might just claim that they haven't received your cancellation letter and you will have no way of proving you sent it.

GYM CONTRACT: Some memberships are for 6, 12 or even 18 months. Don't forget that you will still have to cancel the contract; it doesn't expire automatically but instead rolls over, so don't miss the notice date (usually up to three months before the original date). You should be able to cancel the contract before it expires if you're leaving the country but make sure that option is also in the contract. If it's a gym chain, check if you can use just one or all of their gyms (even abroad).
Again, always send your termination by registered mail.

Useful vocabulary:

Contract	Vertrag
Rental contract	Mietvertrag
Employment contract	Arbeitsvertrag
Insurance contract	Versicherungsvertrag
Mobile phone contract	Handyvertrag
Gym contract	Fitnessstudiovertrag
Customer number	Kundennummer (Kundennr.)
Contract number	Vertragsnummer (Vertragsnr.)
Make a contract	einen Vertrag abschließen
Change (the contract)	(den Vertrag) ändern
The contract expires	der Vertrag läuft aus
The insurance covers	der Versicherung deckt ab
Service	Leistung
Membership	Mitgliedschaft
Member	Mitglied
Sign	unterschreiben
Signature	Unterschrift
The fine print	das Kleingedruckte
Cancel a contract	(einen Vertrag) kündigen
With immediate effect	mit sofortiger Wirkung
As soon as possible	zum nächstmöglichen Zeitpunkt
Notice period	Kündigungsfrist
Contract period	Vertragslaufzeit
Confirmation	Bestätigung
Send by registered mail	per Einschreiben schicken
I'd like to make a contract.	Ich möchte einen Vertrag abschließen.
I'd like to change / cancel my contract.	Ich möchte meinen Vertrag ändern / kündigen.
Can I do that online?	Kann ich das online machen?
What are the services?	Was sind die Leistungen?
What does the insurance cover?	Was deckt die Versicherung ab?
Does the insurance cover this?	Deckt die Versicherung das ab?
What's the contract period?	Was ist die Vertragslaufzeit?
How long is the notice period?	Wie lang ist die Kündigungsfrist?
Where do I have to sign?	Wo muss ich unterschreiben?
Will the contract expire automatically or do I have to cancel?	Läuft der Vertrag automatisch aus oder muss ich kündigen?

I'd like to cancel as soon as possible.	Ich möchte zum nächstmöglichen Zeitpunkt kündigen.
I'd like to send this by registered mail.	Ich möchte das per Einschreiben schicken.
Can I have a confirmation, please?	Kann ich bitte eine Bestätigung haben?

Sample contract cancellation letter:

Peter Smith
Hauptstr. 1
12345 Berlin
Tel.: 0170 / 555 555
Email-Adresse: peter.smith@internet.com

Kundennr.: 9876 5432

Berlin, den 01.01.2020
Sehr geehrte Damen und Herren,

hiermit möchte ich meinen Vertrag zum nächstmöglichen Zeitpunkt / zum 30.04.2020 kündigen.
Bitte senden Sie mir eine Bestätigung der Kündigung.

Mit freundlichen Grüßen
Peter Smith

Customer number: 9876 5432

Dear Sir/Madam,

I would like to terminate my contract at the earliest possible date / on 30.04.2020.
Please send me a confirmation of the termination.

Kind regards,
Peter Smith

Test yourself
Making and canceling contracts
Verträge abschließen und kündigen

1. Ich möchte eine Versicherung abschließen.

a. Woher kommen Sie?
b. Bitte unterschreiben Sie hier.
c. Natürlich, über die Kreuzung und dann links.
d. Natürlich, eine Krankenversicherung?

2. Kann ich per Email kündigen?

a. Nein, nur per Post.
b. Ja, heute.
c. Haben Sie einen Termin?
d. Was ist Ihre Email-Adresse?

3. Wann möchten Sie kündigen?

a. Zum nächstmöglichen Zeitpunkt.
b. Ja, vielen Dank.
c. Im Zentrum.
d. Um acht Uhr.

4. Kann ich das online machen?

a. Ja, per Einschreiben.
b. Nein, Sie müssen unterschreiben.
c. Wo ist das Finanzamt?
d. Ja, oder gestern.

5. Wie lang ist die Kündigungsfrist?

a. Im Sommer
b. 2025
c. 3 Monate
d. Ca. 100 Meter

6. Deckt die Versicherung das ab?

a. Nein, danke.
b. Ja, stimmt so.
c. Ja, das ist alles.
d. Nein, leider nicht.

Answers: 1d, 2a, 3a, 4b, 5c, 6d

CHAPTER 16
At the doctor's / dentist's
Beim Arzt / Zahnarzt

Well, you've put it off and put it off but that pain in your (insert body part of your choice here) isn't going away by itself - despite your best efforts. It's time to suck it up and go see a medical professional. Depending on where you live, there's a good chance you'll find a doctor or dentist who speaks English. However, the reception staff may not. And, as it's your first visit, you'll have to fill in a form with lots of long German medical words. Luckily, a lot of these stem from Latin so will probably be recognizable.

There are a variety of doctors in Germany, from general practitioners to specialists, such as cardiologists and radiologists. If you need to see a specialist, you'll normally be referred by your GP but it's also acceptable to make an appointment directly with the specialist in certain cases.

Surgery opening hours vary but many are open from 8 a.m. to 6 p.m. with a two-hour break in the afternoon. The standard of care in Germany is typically regarded as very good, although there may be long waiting times at busy clinics. If you have German health insurance, your costs will be partly covered. If you're an EU citizen, you can use your European Health Insurance Card (EHIC).

On a final note, it's a good idea to look up your height and weight in centimeters / kilos if you don't know them. Writing "the same height as Kylie Minogue" doesn't really cut it with the rather exacting Germans. But you can give it a try.

FAQ:

How can I find a doctor near me?
Please see the list of useful websites at the back of the book.

Do I have to make an appointment?
Most practices offer a walk-in service (for emergencies) but you could be waiting for a very long time so it's probably best to make an

appointment. You can do this over the phone, in person, or possibly online depending on the practice. But even then you might have to wait.

Do I need a doctor's certificate if I'm too ill to go to work?

Depending on your place of employment, you normally need to get a doctor's certificate after one to three days.

What if I need to see a specialist?
With the exception of a few specialists (gynecologists, ophthalmologists, pediatricians, dentists), you can't just show up or make an appointment directly. Instead you will have to see your general physician first and, if they consider it necessary, they will refer you (*überweisen*) to the specialist. Unfortunately, it can often take weeks or months to get an appointment, depending on the city or area. It might be helpful to ask the GP to give you an urgent referral (*Überweisung mit Dringlichkeitsvermerk*) or contact your insurance company and ask if they can help you get an earlier appointment.

Will my medical insurance cover my visit?
To be on the safe side, you should always ask the doctor or the receptionist if your insurance covers your treatment but, in general, you can assume it will. Some special treatments are not covered by (all) insurances but the doctor should let you know in advance.

Useful vocabulary:

(Filling out the new patient form)	
Patient name	Patientenname / Name des Patienten
Patient address	Adresse / Anschrift
Telephone number	Telefonnummer
Email address	Emailadresse
Date of birth	Geburtsdatum
Gender	Geschlecht
Height	Größe
Weight	Gewicht
Emergency contact	Notfallkontaktnummer / Kontaktinformation für den Notfall
Reason for today's visit	Grund für den Besuch
Allergies	Allergien
Existing conditions (illnesses / intolerances)	Bestehende Krankheiten / Unverträglichkeiten
Place / date	Ort / Datum
Signature	Unterschrift
Doctor	Arzt (male) / Ärztin (female)
General physician	Allgemeinarzt / Hausarzt
Dentist	Zahnarzt
Ophthalmologist / eye doctor	Augenarzt
Dermatologist	Hautarzt
Gynecologist	Frauenarzt / Gynäkologe
Psychiatrist	Psychiater
Psychologist	Psychologe
Receptionist (at a doctor's office)	Sprechstundenhilfe
Consulting hours	Sprechstunde
Examination / check-up	Untersuchung
Treatment	Behandlung
Diagnosis	Diagnose
Pain	Schmerzen
Illness	Krankheit
Arm	Arm
Back	Rücken
Hand	Hand
Finger	Finger
Shoulders	Schultern

Leg	Bein
Tooth / teeth	Zahn / Zähne
Stomach	Magen
Belly	Bauch
Lungs	Lunge
Heart	Herz
Throat / neck	Hals
Skin	Haut
Broken	gebrochen
Fracture	Bruch
Sprained	verstaucht
Headache	Kopfschmerzen
Toothache	Zahnschmerzen
A filling	Füllung
Vomit	erbrechen
Diarrhoea	Durchfall
A cold	Erkältung / Schnupfen
Flu	Grippe
Blood	Blut
Bleeding	bluten
Wound	Wunde
Injury	Verletzung
Infection	Entzündung / Infektion
Allergic reaction	allergische Reaktion
Swollen	geschwollen
Prescription	Rezept
Medicament / drug	Medikament
Pill	Tablette
Cream	Creme / Salbe
Pharmacy	Apotheke
Hello, I have an appointment at…	Hallo, ich habe einen Termin um….
My name is…	Mein Name ist…
It's my first time here.	Ich bin das erste Mal hier.
Where is the waiting room?	Wo ist das Wartezimmer?
Please fill out this form.	Bitte füllen Sie das Formular aus.
Here's my completed form.	Hier ist mein ausgefülltes Formular.
Do you have your health insurance card with you?	Haben Sie Ihre Versichertenkarte dabei?
Here's my health insurance card.	Hier ist meine Versichertenkarte.
Is there a toilet?	Gibt es eine Toilette?

Please take a seat (in the waiting room).	Bitte setzen Sie sich. / Bitte nehmen Sie (im Wartezimmer) Platz.
Wait for your name to be called.	Warten Sie, bis wir sie aufrufen. / Sie werden aufgerufen.
How can I help you?	Wie kann ich Ihnen helfen?
What's the matter?	Was fehlt Ihnen?
Do you have any health problems?	Haben Sie (gesundheitliche) Beschwerden?
What hurts?	Was tut Ihnen weh?
Are you in great pain?	Haben Sie große Schmerzen?
My ... hurts.	Mein .... tut weh.
I have a pain in my ...	Ich habe Schmerzen in meinem....
I'm allergic to....	Ich bin allergisch gegen...

Test yourself
At the doctor's / dentist's

Beim Arzt / Zahnarzt

1. Ich habe einen Termin um 8.

a. Gibt es eine Toilette?
b. Haben Sie einen Termin?
c. Haben Sie Ihre Versichertenkarte dabei?
d. Ich arbeite Vollzeit.

2. Hier ist mein ausgefülltes Formular.

a. Danke, nehmen Sie bitte kurz im Wartezimmer Platz.
b. Nein, danke.
c. Ja, ich habe einen Termin.
d. Haben Sie Beschwerden?

3. Haben Sie Allergien?

a. Heute um 8
b. Ja, ich bin allergisch gegen Erdnüsse.
c. Ja, es ist dringend.
d. Nein, ich brauche ein Rezept.

4. Was tut Ihnen weh?

a. Ich habe Schmerzen.
b. Meine Telefonnummer
c. Mein Finger ist geschwollen.
d. Mein Rücken und meine Schultern

5. Brauchen Sie eine Krankmeldung?

a. Ja, bitte.
b. Bitte am Wochenende
c. Mein Arm ist gebrochen.
d. Nein, ich habe Kopfschmerzen.

6. Was fehlt Ihnen?

a. Ich habe ein Rezept.
b. Ich habe Bauchschmerzen.
c. Ich bin das erste Mal hier.
d. Ich brauche eine Krankmeldung.

Answers: 1c, 2a, 3b, 4d, 5a, 6b

CHAPTER 17
At the post office
Bei der Post

By now, you've been here long enough that your old friends back home are probably rather curious about your new life in Germany. Maybe you'd like to send them a gift - some sexy *Lederhosen* or tasty German sausage, perhaps - to give them an impression of what living here is like. Or maybe they're worried you're starving to death (unlikely) and have sent you a care package from home. Either way, you'll probably have to visit the post office where, chances are, they don't (or won't) speak English.

FAQ:

Do I need to go to the post office just to buy a stamp?
Probably not. A lot of kiosks or newsagents sell stamps so you can just go to your nearest one and ask. Most post offices also have a stamp machine to save you standing in line. Best of all, you can now buy "internet stamps" which you print out yourself. (See back of book.)

Where do I collect my package?
Check on the delivery slip that you found in your mailbox. Often you have to collect it at a post office but sometimes little shops on your street or your neighbors will have accepted it for you.

What do I need to bring with me to collect a package?
The delivery slip and your passport or ID.

Is the German postal service reliable?
It's fairly reliable but of course a letter or package can get lost. A letter mailed during the day is supposed to arrive the next day (within Germany) but often only gets there a day later. And, as in most countries, send packages and cards early around Christmas time.

What does *"Bitte frankieren"* mean?
It means that you have to put a stamp on the letter. But in typically confusing German fashion, sometimes you don't have to; some letters to the *Amt* can be sent without paying postage. These are usually marked with the phrase *"Bitte freimachen falls Marke zur Hand"*, which means it

would be nice if you used a stamp but only if you happen to have one at hand. So... why would you?

I was at home. Why wasn't my package delivered?
Unfortunately, this is quite common but it's often not the fault of the delivery staff. Delivery companies are known to pay poor wages and overload their employees with work. It means that sometimes it's just not possible to deliver all the packages that were stuffed into the van over the course of the day. So, delivery staff often end up delivering the rest of the packages to the post office without coming to your door.

Useful vocabulary:

Post office	Post
Stamp	Briefmarke
Postage	Porto
Envelope	Umschlag
Postcard	Postkarte
Letter	Brief
Parcel	Päckchen
Package	Paket
Delivery	Lieferung
Standard mail	Standard-Versand
Express mail	Eilsendung
Registered mail	Einschreiben
Airmail	Luftpost
Frank	frankieren / freimachen
I'd like to send this, please.	Ich möchte das gerne verschicken.
I'd like to send this by registered mail, please.	Ich möchte das gerne als Einschreiben senden.
How much is the postage?	Was kostet das Porto?
What's the difference in price between ... and ... ?	Was ist der Preisunterschied zwischen... und...?
How long will it take?	Wie lange dauert es?
When will the letter arrive?	Wann kommt der Brief an?
Can I get a receipt for that?	Kann ich einen Beleg dafür bekommen?
I'd like to collect a package, please.	Ich möchte ein Paket abholen.
Here is my delivery slip and ID.	Hier ist die Benachrichtigung und mein Ausweis.

Test yourself
At the post office
Bei der Post

1. Was kostet die Briefmarke?

a. Zusammen oder getrennt?
b. 100 Euro inklusive Nebenkosten
c. 70 Cent
d. Stimmt so.

2. Was ist der Preisunterschied zwischen einem Päckchen und einem Paket?

a. Zwei Euro
b. Möchten Sie ein Paket?
c. Das Porto
d. Das Päckchen ist kleiner.

3. Wie lange dauert es?

a. Morgen Vormittag
b. Circa zwei Tage
c. Möchten Sie einen Beleg?
d. Das ist alles.

4. Ich möchte das als Einschreiben senden.

a. Kann ich Ihren Ausweis sehen?
b. Gerne, das Porto ist 3,79 Euro.
c. Haben Sie einen Termin?
d. Ich bin ledig.

5. Ich möchte ein Paket abholen.

a. Der Rest ist für Sie.
b. Geradeaus und dann links.
c. Haben Sie Ihre Versichertenkarte?
d. Haben Sie eine Benachrichtigung?

6. Was kostet eine Postkarte nach Kanada?

a. 10 Euro mit Beleg
b. 5 Euro mit Benachrichtigung
c. 4 Euro mit Luftpost
d. 8 Euro mit Einbauküche

Answers: 1c, 2a, 3b, 4b, 5d, 6c

CHAPTER 18
At the hairdresser's
Beim Friseur

Putting your crowning glory in the hands of a stranger can be nerve-wracking at the best of times but when you have to try to explain what you want in a language you're not fully familiar with, it can be downright disastrous. Bringing in a few pictures of the style you want can be enormously helpful; being familiar with the metric system is also useful. There's a big difference between five centimeters and five inches so be sure to check your conversions before the snip-snip starts. Walking out of there looking like (a more tearful) Jim Carrey in Dumb and Dumber probably wasn't what you were going for.

So that you don't end up with a mullet - unless you actually want one - the following vocabulary should be more effective than making scissoring gestures with your fingers and hoping.

FAQ:

Are hair salons in Germany expensive?
There are very cheap chains (about €10 for a woman's haircut) but the service might not be great (in and out in 15 minutes). The cheapest option is to dry / style your own hair at the end. More traditional hairdressers might be a bit (to a lot) more expensive but, most of the time, you get what you pay for.

Will the hairdresser try to make small talk?
Hairdressers in the cheaper establishments might prefer to talk to their colleagues instead of paying attention to the customer but others will probably try to engage you in light conversation as it's the traditional way to hear and talk about the latest gossip. If the thought of having to make small talk in German makes you nervous, bring a book or a magazine along.

Should I make an appointment?
It depends on the place. With busy, popular businesses, not making an appointment is frowned upon but in the big cities, where there are so many salons to choose from, most places will happily serve you on the spot. Some cheaper salons even have a machine where you simply take a number and wait your turn.

Do I give a tip? How much?

Please do - hairdressers don't make a lot of money and mostly live off their tips. 10% to 20% is a good idea. Sometimes each hair stylist has a "piggy bank" with their name or picture on it on the reception desk so just pop your tip in there.

Useful vocabulary:

Hairdresser	Friseur (male) / Friseurin (female)
Hair	Haare
Wash	waschen
Cut	schneiden
Blow dry	trocknen / föhnen
Dry your own hair	selbst trocknen
Hair cut	Haarschnitt
Styling	frisieren
Dye (noun)	Farbe
Dye (verb)	färben
Lighter / darker	heller / dunkler
Blonde	blond
Brunette	brünett
Redhaired	rothaarig
Roots	Wurzeln
(Dry) scalp	(trockene) Kopfhaut
Layers	Stufen
Fringe / bangs	Pony
Eye brows	Augenbrauen
Lashes	Wimpern
Pluck	zupfen
Bob	Bob
Highlights	Strähnchen
Beard	Bart
Moustache	Schnurrbart
Sideburns	Koteletten
Trim (verb)	nachschneiden
Cut the ends	Spitzen schneiden
Extensions	Haarverlängerung
Good / bad condition	guter / schlechter Zustand
Split ends	Spliss
Shave	rasieren
Long / short / medium-length	lang / kurz / mittellang
Shampoo / conditioner	Shampoo / Conditioner
Hairspray	Haarspray
Hi, I have an appointment at…	Hallo, ich habe einen Termin um….
My name is …	Mein Name ist...
Hi, I don't have an appointment but is it possible to get a haircut?	Hallo, ich habe keinen Termin, aber kann ich trotzdem jetzt kommen?

I'd like to get highlights.	Ich hätte gern Strähnchen.
How much shall I cut off?	Wie viel soll ich abschneiden?
How much should come off?	Wie viel soll ab?
Just a little off / a trim.	Nur nachschneiden / nur etwas kürzer.
Please cut about 5 cm.	Bitte schneiden Sie circa 5 cm ab.
Please only cut the ends.	Bitte schneiden Sie nur die Spitzen.
The ends are damaged.	Die Spitzen sind kaputt.
I'm going to a wedding / party.	Ich gehe auf eine Hochzeit / Feier.
How long will it take?	Wie lange dauert es?
How long do I have to wait?	Wie lange muss ich warten?
It looks great! Thank you so much!	Das sieht toll aus! Vielen Dank!
Oh my God! That's terrible! You'll be hearing from my lawyer!	Oh Gott! Das ist schrecklich! Sie hören von meinem Anwalt!

Test yourself
At the hairdresser's
Beim Friseur

1. Hallo, ich habe einen Termin um 14 Uhr.

a. Haben sie trockene Kopfhaut?
b. Bitte warten Sie kurz.
c. Möchten Sie Shampoo?
d. Wir haben einen Fahrstuhl.

2. Wie lange muss ich warten?

a. Eine Stunde
b. Eine Monatsmiete
c. Eine Fahrkarte
d. Eine Farbe

3. Möchten Sie Ihre Wimpern färben?

a. Nein danke, ich möchte Kaffee.
b. Ja, bitte, mit Trinkgeld.
c. Nein, nur die Haare schneiden.
d. Ja, und bitte komplett rasieren.

4. Wie viel soll ich abschneiden?

a. Bitte nur etwas kürzer schneiden.
b. Bitte färben.
c. Bitte Strähnchen.
d. Bitte ein Kilo.

5. Waschen und schneiden bitte.

a. Das sieht toll aus!
b. Auch föhnen?
c. Ich bin der Friseur.
d. Das ist alles.

6. Soll ich den Bart rasieren?

a. Nein, nur nachschneiden.
b. Ja, morgen früh.
c. Meine Haare sind hell.
d. Mit Haarspray bitte.

Answers: 1b, 2a, 3c, 4a, 5b, 6a

CHAPTER 19
In the bedroom
Im Schlafzimmer

"Why on earth would I need advice on sleeping?" you ask. "I've been sleeping rather successfully all my life, thank you very much!" That as may be, you haven't been sleeping in a German bedroom all your life and that, friends, is a whole other ball game.

Sleeping in Germany is a serious business - don't be surprised if, when you go back to your new lover's place and are passionately shedding your smalls as you make your way towards the bedroom, you are faced with a bit of a surprise when you get there. You see, practicality trumps romance in a German bedroom. Sure, there's a double bed, but you won't be snuggling up under a double duvet after the main event. *NEIN*, this could lead to all sorts of chaotic behaviour. One of you might get more of the blanket than the other, for instance... On a German double bed, there are usually two single duvets which, when you think about it, actually makes perfect sense.

And what if you like a soft mattress but your partner prefers a firm one? Not to worry - the Germans have you covered there, too. It's pretty common to see two single mattresses on a double bed (at least in more traditional households). In fact, there's even a word for the groove between the two mattresses - *"Besucherritze"* (visitor's gap) - possibly one of the greatest German compound nouns ever invented. Or maybe that title should go to the *Liebesbrücke* (love bridge) you can buy to bridge said gap.

Last but not least - pillows. Probably the one thing that has most foreigners rolling their eyes, raising a confused eyebrow, and shaking their heads in bemusement. You see, pillows in Germany are not your standard rectangular haven of loveliness. No, not content with this, the Germans have created massive square monstrosities that have the approximate consistency of a soggy marshmallow. It doesn't matter how much you fluff them, pile them, or beat them, as soon as you lay your head on a German pillow, the stuffing retreats to all four corners and your head is left languishing pathetically on the mattress.
Why, Germany, just why??

FAQ:

Where can I buy "normal" pillows?

The standard pillow size in Germany is 80cm by 80cm but don't despair - it is possible to find "normal" pillows. IKEA, Karstadt and Primark are probably your best bet, and Dänisches Bettenlager also stock a range of sizes. They've become more and more popular in recent years (for obvious reasons).

Expat tip:
The one good thing about the big square fluffballs is that there's almost always a cold spot somewhere. My American pillow was as thin and hard as a piece of corrugated cardboard, and I've learned that the only important thing about a pillow is that it's cold somewhere.
Amy, USA

What is this "duvet" you speak of and how do I use it?

Germans use a duvet (like a thick quilt) and put it inside a duvet cover, which zips or buttons at the end. The cover is changed and washed regularly but the duvet itself is not. Germans quite enjoy shaking them over their balconies or out their windows to air them so, if you suddenly find yourself covered in fluff on your own balcony, that's the reason. Duvets can be washed if needed though; the same goes for pillows and pillow cases.

What size are standard German beds?

The standard single bed is 90cm x 200cm. However, other bed sizes have become more popular - often even singles opt for 140cm x 200cm. 160cm or even 180cm x 200cm mattresses and beds are also available. But of course if you own such a big bed, you might as well choose the traditional German *Ehebett* (marriage bed) with the two mattresses.

What's a slatted frame?

While boxspring beds have just recently appeared in German furniture shops, traditional beds consist of a main bed frame and a slatted frame which supports the mattress. You often have to buy each part separately - for example, at IKEA - so if you don't want to end up sleeping on the floor, make sure you've got everything you need before you leave the store.

Useful vocabulary:

Bed	Bett
Pillow	Kissen
Duvet / blanket	Bettdecke
Mattress	Matratze
Slatted frame	Lattenrost
Bed linen	Bettwäsche
Bed sheets	Bettlaken
Pillow cover	Kissenbezug
Duvet cover	Bettbezug
Hard / soft	Hart / weich
Double bed	Doppelbett
Single bed	Einzelbett
Pajamas	Pyjama / Schlafanzug
Sleep	schlafen
Fall asleep	einschlafen
Wake up	aufwachen
Go to bed	ins Bett gehen
Sleepy	schläfrig
Tired	müde
Awake	wach
Goodnight	Gute Nacht
Sleep well	Schlaf gut (for one person) / Schlaft gut (for more than one) / Schlafen Sie gut (formal)
Sweet dreams!	Süße Träume!
See you tomorrow morning!	Bis morgen früh!
Sleepy head	Schlafmütze

Test yourself
In the bedroom
Im Schlafzimmer

1. Ich möchte Bettwäsche kaufen.

a. Gute Nacht!
b. Möchten Sie auch Bettlaken?
c. Zusammen oder getrennt?
d. Am Sonntag um 18 Uhr.

2. Ich schlafe nicht gut.

a. Ist die Matratze zu hart?
b. Haben Sie ein Bett?
c. Sind Sie eine Schlafmütze?
d. Hat die Wohnung eine Einbauküche?

3. Wann gehst du ins Bett?

a. Ja, ich gehe ins Bett.
b. Danke, das ist alles.
c. Bis morgen!
d. Um 23 Uhr.

4. Mein Kissen ist zu groß.

a. Wir haben auch kleine Kissen.
b. Möchten Sie ein Kissen?
c. Meine Bettdecke ist groß.
d. Süße Träume!

5. Möchten Sie ein Einzelbett?

a. Nein, ich esse nicht hier.
b. Nein, ein Doppelbett bitte.
c. Das Einzelbett ist nicht gebührenfrei.
d. Die Rechnung bitte.

6. Gute Nacht!

a. Bist du wach?
b. Ich möchte bestellen.
c. Gleichfalls!
d. Guten Abend!

Answers: 1b, 2a, 3d, 4a, 5b, 6c

CHAPTER 20
<u>Further Tips</u>
Weitere Tipps

<u>Using the toilet</u>

Men:
You may have heard rumors, and yes, it's true - German men sit down to pee. There's even a rather fantastic German word for it: *"Sitzpinkeln"*. In restaurants and bars, it's perfectly fine to use the urinals but in a German home, you'd better get used to sitting or you will suffer the anger of the German lady of the house. If you find yourself tossed out on your ear for not taking *Sitzpinkeln* seriously, the only option left to you will be *Wildpinkeln*... (you can probably figure out what that means).

Flushing:
First of all, please do.
German toilets feature different flush options to save water; it's not overly complicated. Be aware that toilet paper is flushed, unlike in some countries. Ladies, don't flush tampons, sanitary towels, diapers, etc. German toilets are good, they're not magical.

<u>TV / Radio Contribution (GEZ)</u>

A week or two after you register your address, you'll receive a little surprise in your mailbox - yep, the lovely folks at *ARD ZDF Deutschlandradio Beitragsservice* have found you (or *GEZ - Gebühreneinzugszentrale* - fee collection headquarters). In Germany, each household (NOT each person in the household) has to pay a contribution towards broadcasting services. Don't own a TV? Never listened to a German radio station? It doesn't matter - everyone* has to pay it. Many Germans aren't particularly happy about it either but it is what it is.

It costs €17.50 a month and you have several payment options: every three months (in the middle or at the start of the month), twice a year, or once a year. You can either set up a direct debit or make a transfer. Direct debit is probably the easiest option so just fill in your bank details and send the form back in the pre-paid envelope. You'll receive a confirmation letter that you've registered within a week or two. Be sure to check if someone else in your household is already paying it - if so, write that on the reverse side of the form. Don't just ignore it - *GEZ* will keep after you, you will be charged retrospectively, and possibly fined.

*Exemptions
Anyone receiving financial help from the state (e.g. unemployed or disabled people, students with federal student loans, etc.) does not have to pay the contribution. You'll find the website to apply for exemption at the back of the book.

WiFi

Be incredibly careful about who you share your WiFi password with. Germany has extremely strict laws when it comes to illegal downloads and fines can run into the thousands. If you have guests, be sure to make them aware of this; if subletting your apartment, it's probably wise to add a clause regarding internet usage to the rental agreement. Maybe your neighbor is having connectivity problems and asks you very sweetly for your WiFi code for a few days. Even if they seem like the nicest person in the world, just say no. Feeling a bit mean in the short-run is probably better than ending up in court in the long-run.

However, if you do get a letter from a lawyer demanding €1000+ for your downloaded version of the latest X-Men movie, don't pay it immediately - contact a lawyer of your own. They are usually able to negotiate a deal (it's become a very fast and standard procedure) which, even including the lawyer's fees, will work out much cheaper - probably less than half the original sum demanded.

Expat tip:
"For reference: *Downloading illegal stuff is illegal.*   *Downloading legal stuff is legal.*   *How you download doesn't matter.*   *Such a hard concept to grasp..."*   Guillaume, France

Public holidays

The number of public holiday days varies by state, with the rich (and Catholic) Bavaria having the most (13) and the poor capital (and a few others) the fewest (10) - you can find a list at the back of the book in the "useful websites" section. Public holidays are the same as Sundays - most shops are closed, public transport runs on a reduced schedule and making noise is frowned upon. Unlike in some countries, in most cases, if the public holiday falls on a weekend, it doesn't carry over to the Monday - you'll just have to wait until the following year to enjoy it.

Biking

Germans pretty much come out of the womb on bicycles so if you want to fit in with the locals, riding a bike is a good place to start. As cycling is so popular, Germany is a bike-friendly place with a decent network of cycle lanes and ample bicycle parking. Having front and back lights on your bike is compulsory; a helmet is not required by law but is a smart idea if you like living. Bicycle theft is pretty common in the bigger cities so if you've got a nice set of wheels, a good lock is essential. You could also consider taking out bicycle insurance (see the list of websites at the back of the book).

Only ride your bike in the cycle lanes or, if there are none, on the road. It should go without saying that you ride in the direction of the traffic but this seems to be a difficult concept for some people to grasp. It's *verboten* (forbidden) to ride on the sidewalk - only children under the age of 8 and the adults who accompany them are allowed to - and you can be fined for doing so (usually €15).

Noise laws

These have been mentioned a couple of times throughout the book but what exactly are they? Well, the funny thing is that nobody actually knows. For a people that are very sensitive to noise, the laws are pretty imprecise. Courts have decided that music should not be played any louder than *Zimmerlautstärke* - i.e. not louder than the normal volume you'd need to hear it in a room, but nobody can clearly state how many decibels this is.

As a general rule, take it that you should be quiet between 10 p.m. and 7 a.m., and also between 1 and 3 p.m, Monday to Saturday. On Sundays and public holidays, be as quiet as possible all the time. It's not unheard of for a neighbor to call the police because of a lawnmower or the click-clack of high heels on a wooden floor.

Allegedly, the noise issue causes around three-quarters of all conflicts between neighbors so, just to be on the safe side, use your common sense and be considerate; being a massive death metal fan doesn't mean everyone else around you is.

Pets

If you want to own a pet in Germany, you'll need to find out if there are any regulations or fees and taxes you have to pay. While cats are tax-free, many communities charge a tax for dogs (*Hundesteuer*) that varies from €10 to €170 per year, depending on where you live. You also need to register your dog, usually at the local tax office (*Steueramt*).

While you're there, ask them if there are any other regulations you need to follow like where to use a leash, how long the leash should be (yep, some places actually have rules for this), and if your breed of dog has to wear a muzzle. You are also obliged to scoop that poop and can be fined if you don't, but mainly do it for the sake of other pedestrians (though unfortunately, many pet owners don't). When renting an apartment, make sure that pets are allowed as many landlords have restrictions.

Greeting Germans

It probably won't come as much of a surprise to learn that the Germans are not the most tactile bunch. They like to keep their distance, especially if they don't know the other person very well. They definitely will not appreciate being hugged or kissed by a person they've just met so keep your arms and lips to yourself - unless you want to see a German run.

It's highly unusual for older people to hug anyone; among younger people it's more common but they still won't hug a stranger. The normal way to greet someone is to shake hands. Later, if you get to know each other better, this might evolve into a friendly hug, which applies to men and women alike. Kisses on the cheek are not popular here - you're in Germany, not France. In general, just wait and see how the other person approaches you and react accordingly.

You might also notice the German love of knocking on tables. For example, if a German man walks into his local bar, instead of shaking everyone's hand, he'll just knock on the table as a greeting; the same on the way out as a goodbye. That way, nobody has to touch anyone, there's no need to worry about germ-transfer (a major phobia here), and everyone still feels acknowledged. Perfect German logic.

Nudity

Maybe you've noticed that, in some regions, the Germans have a very relaxed approach to letting it all hang out. There are lots of nudist beaches, and it's not uncommon to see adults and children running around the many parks and lakes in this beautiful country in their birthday suits. Most spas even impose a ban on wearing swimwear, though you can huddle up under your towel if you want to stick out like a sore thumb.

Of course the Germans have a great name for it - they call it "*Freikörperkultur*" or "*FKK*" (free body culture). This trend originated in East Germany and, even though you can also find *FKK* beaches in the west these days, there is still a big difference between east and west with regards to nudity. So, while you may feel a bit awkward and self-conscious at first, the fact is that some Germans are as comfortable naked as they are in their Jack Wolfskin gear and they're too busy enjoying themselves to be checking out your dangly bits. So go on, live a little!

Expat story:
"I had my first German naked spa experience a few years ago, but I didn't know it was all naked until after I arrived. It is far less scary than you first think. But the plunge pool of ice water is pretty terrible for men. It took me a while to even find certain anatomical things afterwards!"   Kevin, England

Cheap travel in Germany

Train travel in Germany is generally quite expensive, although it is possible to find better deals if you book well before you want to travel (you'll usually find the cheapest fares around 3 months in advance). If you want to travel frequently, you can get a Bahncard which gives you discounts on ticket prices. The options are: Bahncard 25 (for a 25% discount - it costs €62 for one year, 2nd class), 50 (€255 for a 50% discount) or even Bahncard 100 (€4,395) for free travel within Germany. You can get cheaper *Probe*-Bahncards to test them for 3 months which might be useful if you're planning a trip. But don't forget to cancel them on time if you don't want to continue!

The cheapest way to get around, especially when traveling spontaneously, is usually by bus. Flixbus has an extensive number of routes around Germany, tickets are normally very reasonable and, most of the time, the WiFi even works. (See the list of websites at the back of the   book.)

PHONETICS CHART

VOWELS

There is usually a long and a short version of each vowel:

written	sound	pronounced	examples
a (often followed by a double consonant)	short a	like in "*bat*" (British pronunciation)	kann, machen, Hallo
aa, ah, a	long a	like in "*car*"	fahren, Bahn, Name
e (often followed by a double consonant)	short e	like in "*get*"	Bett, hell,
ee, eh, e	long e	no exact equivalent in English, similar to "*fair*"	geht, sehr, leer
i (often followed by a double consonant)	short i	like in "*it*"	stimmt, bitte, Kissen
ie, ih, i	long i	like in "*feel*"	sieben, viel, hier
o (often followed by a double consonant)	short o	like in "*not*"	kommen, Roller, wollen
oo, oh, o	long o	no exact equivalent in English, similar to "*so*" but doesn't glide off into u sound	Wohnung, Note,
u	short u	like in "*foot*"	Mutter, Bus,

(often followed by a double consonant)			
uh, u	long u	like in *"boot"*	gut, Kuchen,

Umlaut (sound alteration vowels)

written	sound	pronounced	examples
äh, ä	long ä	exactly like long e	Käse, ungefähr
ä (often followed by a double consonant)	short ä	exactly like short e	hätte, fährt, Anhänger
öh, ö	long ö	practice: pronounce the long e like in *"Lesung"* and then purse your lips, so that the word turns into *"Lösung"*	Größe
ö (often followed by a double consonant)	short ö	shorter and more open version of the long ö	möchten, geöffnet
üh, ü, y	long ü	practice: pronounce the long i like in *"Tier"* and then purse your lips, so that the word turns into *"Tür"*	für, Grüße, Führerschein
ü, y (often followed by a double consonant)	short ü	shorter version of the long ü	München, Küche

Diphthongs (double vowels)

written	pronounced	examples
au	like in "*now*"	Frau, kaufen, Auge
eu, äu	like in "*toy*"	Euro, Gebäude, Steuer
ei	like in "*by*"	nein, Feiertag, Bein

CONSONANTS
The consonants that are not mentioned here have no special pronunciation

written	pronounced	examples
b	1. at the beginning of a word or syllable pronounced like /b/ 2. at the end of a word or syllable pronounced like /p/	1. **B**erlin 2. a**b**
ch	1. following the vowels a, o, u, au like in "*Lo**ch** Ness*" (throaty sound) 2. following the vowels e, i, ä, ö, ü, eu, äu, ei similar to the /h/ sound in "*huge*"	1. nach, kochen, Buch, auch 2. Rechnung, ich, möchten, euch, leicht
d	1. at the beginning of a word or syllable pronounced like /d/ 2. at the end of a word or syllable pronounced like /t/	**D**eutschlan**d**
g	1. at the beginning of a word or syllable pronounced like /g/ 2. at the end of a word or syllable pronounced like /k/	**g**uten Ta**g**
j	like in "yes"	ja, jeden, Jahr
qu	like /kv/	Quote, überqueren
r	1. at the beginning of a word	1. Radio, rot, Rest

	or syllable, rolling sound in the back of the throat, like gargling 2. after any vowels, pronounced like a little /a/	2. Wasser, Berlin, Ohr, nur, Bar
s	1. at the beginning of a word or syllable pronounced like "*zone*" 2. at the end of a word or syllable pronounced like "*so*"	1. Saft, so, Soße, Nase 2. aus, fast, Lust
ss, ß (not used in Switzerland and Liechtenstein)	like in "*so*"	heißen, essen, Straße
sch	like in "*short*"	schön, Schmerzen, zwischen
st	1. at the beginning of a word or syllable pronounced like /sht/ 2. at in the end of a word or syllable pronounced like /st/	1. Stadt, Tankstelle, Station 2. fast, hast, ist
sp	like /shp/	Spanien, Sport, sprechen
v	like /f/	viel, vier, verheiratet
w	like in "*vain*"	wo, Wohnung, Wein
z	like /ts/	zahlen, Zahn, Zürich

USEFUL LINKS

Chapter 1: The basics
Dictionaries:
dict.leo.org/german-english/
www.linguee.de
And of course - translate.google.com

Chapter 3: Finding an apartment
Popular apartment-search websites:
www.immobilienscout24.de
www.immowelt.de
www.deutsche-wohnen.com
www.wg-gesucht.de (shared accommodation)

Credit rating report: www.meineschufa.de/
Credit rating report: https://bonitaetscheck.immobilienscout24.de/

Finding the local Mietverein: https://www.mieterbund.de

Comparison website for personal liability insurance:
www.check24.de/privathaftpflicht

Chapter 4: At the Bürgeramt
Finding your local Bürgeramt - www.behoerdenfinder.de

Book an appointment / download forms
Berlin: service.berlin.de/terminvereinbarung/
Munich: -
https://www.muenchen.de/rathaus/terminvereinbarung_bb.html
Hamburg: https://netappoint.de/hamburg/?company=hamburg
Cologne: https://www.stadt-koeln.de/service/termine-online-vereinbaren

Or call 115 (nationwide).

Chapter 5: Opening a bank account
Bank comparison: https://www.check24.de/girokonto/

Chapter 6: Health insurance
Artists' insurance: https://www.kuenstlersozialkasse.de/kuenstler-und-publizisten/voraussetzungen.html

Chapter 7: Taxes
Lists of income tax rates: https://einkommensteuertabellen.finanz-tools.de/
Find a Finanzamt - https://www.finanzamt24.de/
Unofficial tax calculator:
 https://www.steuergo.de/en/rechner/brutto_netto_rechner
Termination of church membership: https://www.kirchenaustritt.de/
Online tax declaration: https://www.elster.de/eportal/start

Chapter 10: Driving
List of countries with agreements for exchanging licences:
https://www.adac.de/-/media/adac/pdf/jze/staatenliste-nicht-eu-land-umtausch-fuehrerschein.pdf

Chapter 11: Recycling
Buy or sell used items: https://www.ebay-kleinanzeigen.de/
Find recycling centers for bulky waste:
http://recyclinghof.net/recyclinghof_bundesland_deutschland.html

Chapter 12: In a restaurant / bar / café
Smoking laws:
https://en.wikipedia.org/wiki/Smoking_in_Germany#Smoking_ban_by_state

Chapter 14: Children
Form to apply for child support:
https://www.kindergeld.org/formulare.html
Government childcare finder:
https://www.bmfsfj.de/doku/Publikationen/kinderbetreuungsboerse/
Find a Kita: https://www.kita.de/

Chapter 15: Making and canceling contracts
Check mobile reception (three main providers):
Telekom: https://www.telekom.de/start/netzausbau
O2: https://www.o2online.de/service/netz-verfuegbarkeit/netzabdeckung/
Vodafone: https://www.vodafone.de/hilfe/netzabdeckung.html

Chapter 16: At the doctor's / dentist's
Find a medical practitioner: https://www.med-kolleg.de/docsearch/
Find a late-night pharmacy:
https://www.aponet.de/service/notdienstapotheke-finden.html (just enter your postal code)

Chapter 17: At the post office

Find a branch / postbox: https://www.deutschepost.de/de.html
Buy stamps: https://shop.deutschepost.de/shop/internetmarke
Track a DHL package: https://www.dhl.de/en/privatkunden/dhl-sendungsverfolgung.html

Chapter 20: Further tips

Public holidays by state: https://publicholidays.de/2019-dates/
Bicycle insurance: https://www.bike-ass.de/
Application for exemption of GEZ contribution:
https://www.rundfunkbeitrag.de/buergerinnen_und_buerger/formulare/be
freiung_oder_ermaessigung_beantragen/index_ger.html
Train tickets and bahncard: www.bahn.de
Flix bus: https://global.flixbus.com/

Other useful websites:

Local news in English:
thelocal.de
https://www.dw.com/en/

Getting settled in Germany:
Expatica.com
Expath.de
https://www.howtogermany.com/

Useful information:
https://www.iamexpat.de/